ECHOES FROM EDEN

Echoes

from

Eden

A.W. Tozer

Edited by Gerald B. Smith

CHRISTIAN PUBLICATIONS
CAMP HILL, PENNSYLVANIA

Christian Publications
3825 Hartzdale Drive, Camp Hill, PA 17011

Faithful, biblical publishing since 1883

ISBN: 0-87509-566-6
LOC Catalog Card Number: 94-68314
© 1981, 1994 by Christian Publications
All rights reserved
Printed in the United States of America

94 95 96 97 98   5 4 3 2 1

Cover photo © by Jonathan L. Graf

Echoes from Eden is also in print with KJV references as
part of the *The Tozer Pulpit*.

CONTENTS

PREFACE

The ministry of Dr. A.W. Tozer is frequently identified by his gift that urges believers to press into all the possibilities of the grace of God. But in his zeal to bring Christians to maturity, Tozer never neglected the basic themes of the gospel. An unbeliever could not hear his sermons or read his writings without learning something about the way back to God. Dr. Tozer's gift as an evangelist is often overlooked. In this series Tozer explores the mercy of God in calling sinners to repentance and salvation.

Beginning in the garden of Eden, the voice of the Creator sounded out to Adam a clear invitation to return from the path of disobedience. That loving call has been echoing and reechoing ever since. God has spoken and He is now speaking to men through the voice of love, the voice of the Holy Spirit, the voice of conscience, the voice of the soul, the voice of reason, the voice of Jesus' blood, the voice of accountability and the voice of judgment.

The theology of the calling of God has seldom been better stated than in these messages by the church in our day. At a time when Madison

1

Avenue methodology and doctrinal fuzziness have taken over so much of contemporary evangelism, it is essential to restate in biblical terms the divine calling of man by his Creator and Savior. Anyone concerned about true evangelism will find these studies sharpening his understanding of the basic issues the soul-winner must confront.

A Sick Planet without Meaning:
A Fallen Race without God

But the LORD God called to the man, "Where are you?" (Genesis 3:9)

Although the human mind stubbornly resists and resents the suggestion that it is a sick, fallen planet upon which we ride, everything within our consciousness, our innermost spirit, confirms that the voice of God is sounding in this world—the voice of God calling, seeking, beckoning to lost men and women!

At first thought, the human being wonders why it should be necessary for the divine voice of entreaty to be heard at all in the earth.

There is only one possible answer, it can only be because we are out of the way, lost and alienated from God. Even the very world we inhabit is a lost world.

There are many reasons to believe that the earth

upon which we ride is a lost planet. Hints of this are found throughout the entire Bible, and through the anointed intellect such evidences may be found also in nature.

After the great failure of our first parents, God said this about our planet as He spoke to Adam and Eve:

> Cursed is the ground because of you; . . .
> It will produce thorns and thistles for
>   you . . .
> until you return to the ground,
>   since from it you were taken;
> for dust you are
>   and to dust you will return.
>   (Genesis 3:17-19)

Now, why were those words ever spoken?

I believe they were spoken to describe the planet which is our habitation. We have our clue here that it is a lost planet.

I would quote here also from the writings of a man of profound intellect, the Apostle Paul. I believe that it would be generally conceded in most circles that Paul possessed one of the most brilliant and profound minds that ever set a pen to paper.

This is the passage from the eighth chapter of the book of Romans, the quotation taken from the British Williams translation:

> This world of nature was condemned to

> be without meaning, not by its own will
> but by the will of him who condemned
> it, in the hope that not only mankind but
> this world of nature also might be set
> free from bondage to decay, to enter the
> glorious liberty of sons of God. For to
> this day, as you know, the whole world
> of nature cries out in pain like a woman
> in childbirth. (8:20-22)

So, long before our time, this world of nature was condemned to exist without meaning, that is, "vanity". Perhaps it is not strange that the very words that the philosophers like to use are used here by the sacred writer—that nature is without meaning! And yet there is a glorious promise here as well—giving hope that not only mankind but this world of nature is to be set free from bondage to decay.

But there is something worse than the fact that this is a sick, fallen planet and that is the truth that the inhabitants of this planet are also lost.

We believe that God created us living souls and gave us bodies through which we can experience the world around us and communicate with one another. When man fell through sin, he began to think of himself as having a soul instead of being one. It makes a lot of difference whether a man believes that he is a body having a soul or a soul having a body!

For the moral "unlikeness" between man and God the Bible has a word—alienation. The Holy

Spirit presents a frightful picture of this alienation as it works itself out in human character. Fallen human nature is precisely opposite to the nature of God as revealed in Jesus Christ. Because there is no moral likeness there is no communion, hence the feeling that God is far away in space.

Lost, But Not Abandoned

Yet when we speak of men being far from God we speak truly. The Lord said of Israel, "Their hearts are far from me"(Isaiah 29:13), and there we have the definition of "far" and "near" in our relation to God. The words refer not to physical distance, but to likeness.

Actually, men are lost but not abandoned. That is what the Holy Scriptures teach and that is what the Christian Church is commissioned to declare. For any who may doubt it, let me ask, just in the name of reason: does it seem reasonable to you that unique human beings, made in God's image, should each be given just one little turn at bat?

I know also, of course, that there is a theology, or a color or complexion of theology, that squirms uneasily as soon as you say something good about mankind. Many are prepared to say that you are a liberal at the least, if you say something good about mankind.

It is my studied opinion that except for sin, it would be very difficult to overpraise human beings. Consider what we are and what we know and what we can do: our memories, imaginations, artistic abilities, sensibilities and potentialities.

When you thoughtfully consider it, you cannot justly and properly sell mankind short! Sin, God knows, is like a cancer in the heart of a man's being. It ruins the man and damns him at last!

But the man is not all sin, for man was made in the image of God. It is true that sin has ruined him and condemned him to death forever unless he is redeemed through the blood of Jesus. Yet man as a being is only one degree removed from the angels and in some ways is superior indeed to the angels.

Again I ask: does it seem reasonable to you that if this were not a lost world that such a being as man—a Shakespeare or a Churchill or an Edison or any of the great thinkers and writers, artists or engineers—should, like a little kid, be given his one little turn at bat and then be told to sit down while the ages roll on?

Does it seem reasonable to you that a being so Godlike as man should take all of this marvelous comprehension and ability only toward the grave? Should he carry his memory gifts, his brilliant imagination, his artistic creative powers and all those gifted traits that make him a man only to the grave?

Would the Creator God waste His time on such a being as He has made man to be, only to say, "I was just fooling around with man. I just made this marvelous creature for a short day. I am just having some fun!"

That does not seem reasonable to me.

Why does man as we know him consistently live beneath his own ideals? Why is he everlastingly far below what he knows he ought to be? Why is a man doomed to go to the grave frustrated and disappointed at last, never having attained his highest ideals?

You cannot tell me that mankind does not continue to dream of a shining world beyond him. Every man secretly believes that shining world is somewhere there before him—yet nevertheless it is always lost to that man or he is lost to it.

Even those followers of Jesus in His day on earth confessed: "Lord, we don't know where you are going, so how can we know the way?" (John 14:5).

No truer words were ever uttered by any man on this earth! Sacred revelation declares plainly that the inhabitants of the earth are lost. They are lost by a mighty calamitous visitation of woe which came upon them somewhere in that distant past and is still upon them.

But it also reveals a glorious fact—that this lost race has not been given up!

A Divine Voice Calls

There is a divine voice that continues to call. It is the voice of the Creator, God, and it is entreating them. Just as the shepherd went everywhere searching for his sheep, just as the woman in the parable went everywhere searching for her coin, so there is a divine search with many variations of the voice that entreats us, calling us back.

If we were not lost, there would be no Father's voice calling us to return, calling us back. So, I say again that we have not been given up.

Think of the Genesis account: Adam fleeing from the face of God, hiding among the trees of the garden. It was then that the sound of God's gentle voice was heard, saying "[Adam,] where are you?" (Genesis 3:9).

I would remind you that His seeking voice has never died out. The echo of that voice is sounding throughout the widening years. It has never ceased to echo and reecho from peak to peak, from generation to generation, from race to race, and continent to continent, and off to islands and back to the continent again. Throughout all of man's years, "Adam, where are you?" has been the faithful call.

There are many voices, but it is really only one voice.

When a child is lost in the swamp or in the woods, searching parties are organized immediately.

Who is back of that organized search? Is it not the throbbing, anguished heart concern of the mother and father? They have encouraged the officers and the volunteers to hover overhead with helicopters, to send out sound trucks, to organize soldiers, and Boy Scouts, and friendly neighbors—always calling, calling, calling.

There will be many voices calling. It may be the voice of a soldier, a deputy, a volunteer, a neighbor—but always it is in a true sense the father's voice. All of the voices are simply overtones of the same loving father's voice that organized the search and whose distraught heart is calling for his lost child.

So it is with the voice of God! Actually, many voices call us. But it is all one voice.

Man may hear the voice of God's love or the voice of Jesus' blood or the voice of conscience; it may be the voice of the dead or the voice of the living or the voice of the lost or the voice of the saved. Whatever the voice, it is only another inflection of the voice of the One who calls.

It is the distraught heart of God seeking His lost race; calling men and women in any way that He can call them.

He may call from above or from below; He will likely call from around the bend or from down the road or beside the river or on the plateau.

Yes, it is the voice of God entreating us, searching us out and always calling us to return home!

One of Our Greatest Mistakes: Measuring God's Love by Our Own

The LORD appeared to us in the past, saying: "I have loved you with an everlasting love; I have drawn you with loving-kindness. (Jeremiah 31:3)

Perhaps the greatest mistake we humans make is in our insistence upon trying to measure the love of God by our own human standards of love.

As men and women, is it not true that we are most likely to love people for what they are—often for their good behavior?

Let me describe for you what is likely to happen when you tell a sinner that "God really loves you!" That person will say, "I don't believe that."

You see, he can only measure the love of God by his own kind of love.

"I know better than to believe that," he will say.

"I know what I am on the inside. I have lied. I have cheated. I have stolen. There probably is not a sin that I have not committed, either overtly or in my heart. I am worse than anyone knows, so if God is the moral God the Bible says He is, He cannot love me!"

At this point, we must say that he is right, and also that he is wrong.

He is right if he believes that God cannot love him for his sin's sake. But he is wrong because he fails to see that he is loved of God and for God's own sake. He is wrong if he fails to believe that God can love anyone, no matter how sinful, for His own sake and for His Son's sake.

The Love of God

Here are a few things about the love of God that you are not hearing very often in these days.

God, being the divine person that He is, must love Himself first, because His love is a pure and blameless and perfect love.

Please do not say: "Mr. Tozer, you do not really mean that!"

That is exactly what I mean: that God, being Himself God, an uncreated being, deriving from no one, owing nothing to anybody, must necessarily be the fountain of all the love there is! That is why I say that as our God, He must love Himself forever with pure and perfect love.

This kind of love, God's love, holy and blameless—this is the love which the three Persons of the Godhead feel and hold for one another. The Father to the Son; the Son to the Father; the Father and Son to the Spirit; the Spirit to the Father and Son—the divine Trinity in perfect and blameless and proper love; loving one another with a holy, poured out devotion! The Trinity's three fountains, eternal, infinite, pouring without measure into each other from the bottomless, boundless, shoreless sea of perfect love and bliss.

This, I say, is the love of God for His own holy self. God being who and what He is, is Himself the only being that He can love directly. Everything else and everyone else that God loves, He loves for His own sake.

That is why we can believe and say that God loves Himself—and that when it comes to His creatures, His divine or perfect love cannot fall directly upon any man. God must find something of Himself there in order that He may love it. God can only love Himself and that which is like Himself. If God should love and cherish anything unlike Himself, it would be equivalent in our knowledge to a pure and holy woman loving and cherishing an evil man, perhaps a murderous gangster.

God must love that which is equal to Himself and like Himself.

So, when God looks at the mute creation that the translator calls the world of nature, He loves it because it reveals to Him something of the glory and power of His own Godhead. It shows something of His own wisdom.

When God looks on His sun and His moon and all the stars that He has made, His lakes and His rivers, His mountains and His seas, God loves them because they remind Him of His own wisdom and power that gave them being. But when God looks at the seraphim and the cherubim and the holy angels before the throne, He loves them because they remind Him of His own holiness. They are holy angels and their holiness is derived from God. God loves in them that which came from Himself. God can properly and with moral propriety love the holy angels because they are holy beings.

Now, when God considers men and women, He loves in them the fallen relic of His own image!

It is at this point that I seem to be in trouble with a lot of people who write to me and abuse me and insist that I am a liberal.

But I do not have education to be a modernist and I am not a liberal. I believe that the Bible says what God wanted it to say, and it is plain in the Scriptures that the living and eternal God made man in His own image. Therefore, when Jesus Christ was incarnated He came to us in the body of a man—without embarrassment and without change.

"How can that be?" we ask.

Because man was an image of the God who created him; the image of that God who said, "Let us make man in our image" (Genesis 1:26).

Yet, that man is fallen—and that brings in another element here, a foreign element that has crept in. It is the element of man's sin! It is the deadly sting of the serpent, going back to the scene of failure in the garden. That is why man, made in the image of God, is now a dying man; sick unto death because of sin which like the poison of an adder has gotten into his moral veins.

But extract that sin and take it out and you have the image of God again, and Jesus Christ was the true image of God because He was a man without sin.

That is Bible Truth—no modernism there; no liberalism there!

Those who deny that fallen man bears upon him something of the original potential of what he once was are not true friends of the Bible. They themselves are guilty of taking liberties with the Holy Scriptures.

It is still true that when God looks on a sinner and loves the sinner, never while the stars burn in their silence can it be said that God loves the sin in the sinner. Never can it be said that a holy God loves an unholy thing.

And yet God loves sinners—bringing the often repeated question, "Why?"

God loves them for that which He sees in them of His lost and fallen image, for God can never love anything but Himself directly!

Loves for His Own Sake

God loves everything else for His own sake.

You are loved of God, but you are loved of God for the sake of the holy Son, Jesus, who is the Godhead incarnate, who is the second person of the Godhead, the Word who became flesh and dwelt among us. God sees in Jesus Christ what you would have been: that is, He sees that in His perfect humanity, not His deity. You and I could never be divine in that sense.

This is why God loves lost men. He loves them not by the excusing of their sin; not by taking an attitude of carelessness; not by any willingness on His part to become morally lax—but He loves them because He once stood and said, "Let us make man in our image."

Here is an illustration that could fall within our own human experience. A man and a woman meet. After falling in love, they marry and have one child, a son.

They have a great deal of pleasure as they consider the boy's features. Each says that he looks like the other. Then they change it around and insist that he looks like this one—then again, that one. But the child is their son, and they try to see each other in that boy!

The years pass and the boy grows up and approaches manhood. The hour comes when he breaks with society. He chooses to go outside the law. He drinks, gambles, lies, steals, cheats—and then he murders. He becomes a fugitive from justice, known to be vicious and cruel.

The father of that lad dies before the outlaw is caught and thrown into prison. But the grieving mother goes to see him. She knows he is finished. Evidence of every kind is against him, fingerprints everywhere, a thousand witnesses. He will pay for his crimes.

The mother looks through the bars. It is her son standing there, now a full-grown man. Can she love his cruel deeds as an outlaw? Can she love those heartless acts of gangsterism? Does she love his cold-eyed cruelty? No! She hates them with everything in her good heart. But as he stands there, cornered and silent, she sees beyond him in her memory the man who is no longer with her, and she thinks, "If only he had been a good boy—he would have just been the image of his father."

She pours out her heart in tears, doesn't she? She loves the boy—but she does not love one thing in him that made him an outlaw! She loves the image of the man she loved and to whom she gave herself with the promise to follow until the separation by death.

We know that God looks down at the human race and sees us in our awful sin. The Apostle Paul has recorded seventeen deeds which he describes as the works of the flesh—but they are only the beginning. It would take many sheets of paper to write down the long and dreadful list of sins that man has been capable of committing and is still doing. God is still looking and He hates jealousy, deception, lying, gluttony, uncleanness, impurity, outlawries, cruelty.

We cannot ever think that God loves sinners carelessly, loosely, foolishly, with the thought: "I don't care—I love them anyway!" No, I think it is plain that He loves them because He sees in them the image of what Adam was and what Christ is and loves them redemptively now for Jesus' sake.

In the light of God's love and grace, no man ought to strut down the street, proudly professing, "God loves me—I am a fundamentalist!"

Careful, careful!

Your sins have violated and lost to you every right you ever had to be loved by God. But God sees that you are of the loins of the man who once stood up on the earth and looked about for a helpmeet. He was made in the image of God and God was not ashamed of him. And now God sees an image of the man who went to the tree and died between heaven and earth—His only begotten Son.

So, God loves you for reasons other than who you are and what you are. Therefore, humble yourself—it will pay!

How we ought to thank God for the love that comes to us mediated through the Man, Christ Jesus. That everlasting love that is not only everlasting in its object but everlasting in its own quality!

God must love and will love man until hell has erased the last trace of the remaining image. Men are lost now—that we dare not forget. But they are still loved of God, and the man with the worst record is still dear to God for Jesus' sake, because Jesus died on that tree for lost men everywhere.

We cannot get away from God's words of old: "I have loved you with an everlasting love" (Jeremiah 31:3). That love is everlasting because it is the eternal God who loves.

Now, consider the fact that God no longer loves the devil.

There was a day when God loved the devil as He now loves the angels and archangels, because He saw in that created being traces and proofs of His own wisdom. Although not an image of Himself in the sense that man is, the devil was called the covering cherub, of whom God said, "My wisdom and beauty were created in you in the day you were created" (paraphrase of Ezekiel 28:13).

Before his utter rebellion against his Creator, the devil was loved because he was a reflection of what God could do and an evidence of His moral artistry and His omniscient skills. But the devil sinned—and he sinned in some way that erased forever everything within him of which God could be proud.

It is for that reason that God can no longer love the devil. He sent no redeemer for him, for there is not anything in Satan that can remind God of Himself. The last trace of that which might have reminded God of Himself has been washed out in the filthy bilge water of iniquity as century has been added to centuries.

God's Love for the Lost

Believing that, I have long thought upon the continuing love of God for lost men and women for whom Christ died. I share with you a speculation about the future, and because it is speculation you do not have to agree with me. But I believe the time will come when God will no longer love lost human beings!

I believe that God now loves all lost men. There

are lost men in jails and prisons and insane asylums. They are in bars and houses of ill fame and in all circumstances and environments. And God loves them all because the last trace of response has not been erased. He still remembers them and remembers His Son on the tree, suffering in a body like theirs.

He still remembers that the second Person of the divine Being was incarnated in the Man who has a body like that man, yet without sin.

The Bible says the day is coming when "[he] who does wrong [will] continue to do wrong; . . . [he] who is vile [will] continue to be vile; . . . [he] who does right [will] continue to do right; and . . . [he] who is holy [will] continue to be holy" (Revelation 22:11).

Therefore, the day will come when lost men will no longer be loved by God Almighty; for God must love everything for His own sake if He is to continue to be God.

We must face the fact that when a human has sold himself out to sin and the mutilating power of iniquity has wrought to make him to be a devil and not a man, God will no longer love the lost man.

Further, it must be said that we ought not to imagine for a second that God will be pining over hell and grieving in His heart over lost men in hell. That cannot be true! God grieves over lost men now because man can still pray and believe and hope and dream and aspire, so there is still something that reminds Him of the Man who died on the tree.

But when that is all gone, there will be nothing left upon which God can pour out His love. There will no longer be any image, no response and no reception of that love. Therefore, the love of God though everlasting in its source, will no longer light upon fallen man.

Let me point out another fact to you that wherever there is love there has to be good will, as well. As a rule, people will never do anything really bad to those they genuinely love. Love is always accompanied by good will, and I think it is true to say that God is inflamed with good will.

We have read in the newspapers once in a while about the kind of man who will kill a woman because she looked at another man and his excuse to the court is: "I loved her so much that I killed her!"

True love never killed anyone! Love never willed ill or evil to anyone. Love must always have with it good will—and God is inflamed with good will. This means that whatever we think of Him, God is always thinking about us. When the angels sang their song or uttered their marvelous chant it was the message of "good will toward men" (Luke 2:14, KJV).

But you try to tell the sinner that God loves him and that God is inflamed with good will toward him and he will express his doubts about it because he measures love only by his own human experience.

It takes quite a grasp of theology to make people see and understand that God does not love them because they are trying to be good. Many seem to

believe that God must love them because they try
to cultivate good habits; they have always pleased
their mother and father; they have had good
marks in school. Their attitude seems to be: "I can
sort of understand how God can love me."

The truth is that God does love you—but for
another reason altogether. He loves you because
He sees even in you some trace of that glory that
once walked in the garden. Though lost and
ruined by the Fall and on your way to hell, God
loves you for His own sake and not for your sake!

God's love is unique in this universe, for He
loves us for His own sake. Where there is this kind
of love, there is good will, and there is also yearn-
ing!

Who but our God could tell us, "I have drawn
you with loving-kindness" (Jeremiah 31:3)?

He draws us toward Himself. To a lost race and
a lost world there is a clear call from God. There is
nothing that can stand in the way: not character,
reputation, the past—nothing can stand in the way
except our own sin.

God calls you to turn around. He calls you to
make a moral "about face." He calls you to throw
yourself on His mercy. Do not come expecting to
bring a lot of character witnesses to tell God how
good you are. Come just as the prodigal son came
home, willing to confess: "Father, I have sinned"
(Luke 15:21).

Would you ask God sincerely to draw your heart
from earth away; would you ask Him to speak to
your inmost soul and tell you once more: "I am

your love. I am your God. I am your all"?

The voice of God's love continues to entreat you—that mighty love that is equal to God Himself, calling you back to the cross and back to the forgiveness in the Father's house.

CHAPTER 3

The Presence of the Holy Spirit: A Silent, Holy, Eloquent Witness

When he comes, he will convict the world of guilt in regard to sin and righteousness and judgment. (John 16:8)

The Holy Spirit, whom Jesus also called the Spirit of Truth, has not come into this world to fool around. He will be found wherever the Lord's people meet, and in confirming the Word and the Person of Jesus Christ, He will demand moral action!

It is for that reason that when a man goes to a gospel meeting he never knows when the last shred of excuse will be stripped from his naked, trembling conscience forever. Men may joke and play—even about sacred and spiritual matters—but the Spirit of God is in dead earnest!

God is still speaking in this lost world and one of
His voices is the presence of the Holy Spirit, con-
victing a lost human race of such weighty matters
as sin, righteousness, and judgment. While the
Holy Spirit continues in His ministries, we know
that this lost world is not yet a forsaken world.

We have said that God is speaking to mankind
with more than one voice, but it must be said that
the clearest, most distinct and most easily distin-
guished voice is that of the Holy Spirit. The call
and reproof and conviction by the Holy Spirit give
grave and serious meaning to all other voices calling men home.

If it were not for the presence of the Holy Spirit
speaking through the consciences of men and
women, no other voice would have any significance. For the Holy Spirit, the divine Comforter, came to confirm Christ's words and Christ's
work and Christ's person.

Confirm the Words

Now the words of the Lord Jesus Christ were
words so lofty and so filled with authority that no
other religious teacher in history could ever match
His teachings. Other teachers have established
their religious systems, some major and many of
them minor, but the words and teachings of Jesus
are in a class by themselves.

Frankly, the claims that He made brand Him immediately as being God—or an idiot! The
authoritative claims He made outstrip the claims
of all other religious teachers in the world.

Of His own body He said, "Destroy this temple, and I will raise it again in three days" (John 2:19). He told His hearers, "I saw Satan fall like lightning from heaven" (Luke 10:18). He declared with authority, "Before Abraham was born, I am!" (John 8:58). He predicted that

> When the Son of Man comes in his glory, and all the angels with him, he will sit on his throne in heavenly glory. All the nations will be gathered before him, and he will separate the people one from another as a shepherd separates the sheep from the goats. (Matthew 25:31-33).

No one else has ever been able to say, "Do not be amazed at this, for a time is coming when all who are in their graves will hear [my] voice and come out" (John 5:28-29).

No one else has ever talked like that!

So, the Holy Spirit has come as a silent, penetrating, immediate witness of the words of Christ. And the penetrating stillness of the divine Spirit is more terrible than the loudest shout from the housetop.

Yes, the Holy Spirit is here confirming the words of Jesus, and that is why the critics are all in confusion. That is why God immediately makes a fool of the man who becomes a doubter and begins to try to pull the Word of God apart. God withdraws the inner life from such a man so that when he speaks, he speaks as a fool, because the penetrating voice of the Holy Spirit is not heard in his words.

Confirm the Works

The Holy Spirit is also among us to confirm to the consciences of men the works of Jesus.

There was no denying that in His earthly ministry, Jesus was a mighty worker of miracles. He did raise the dead. He did cleanse the leper. He did turn the water into wine. He did feed the multitude with a few pieces of bread.

The Pharisees did not try to deny the miracles He wrought. They could not deny them—for the man who was blind only moments before was now walking among them, with full vision. You cannot deny a fact that stands and stares you in the face—a fact that you can touch and feel and push around and investigate! The Pharisees simply said: "He does his work in the power of the devil."

The Holy Spirit came that He might confirm and verify the divine quality of those mighty works of Jesus and prove Him indeed to be the very God who had made the world and who could make it do what He pleased for it to do.

Confirm the Person

Then there is the confirmation of the person of Christ, the most significant, the most telling force that ever lived in the world, standing head and shoulders above all the great in history. The Holy

Spirit came to do a confirmatory work and He raised Him from the dead and since this mysterious witness is come, Jesus Christ is no longer on trial. It is no longer a question of "Was Jesus the Son of God?"

The Holy Spirit has taken that out of the realm of polemics and has put it in the realm of morals. The silent, immediate witness, this penetrating voice in the conscience of men tells us that this Person was indeed the very Son of God.

As soon a Peter was filled with the Holy Spirit, he immediately stood and preached what he had never preached before; namely, that this man whom they had crucified was the Christ of God, raised from the dead to be Lord and Christ.

Then, too, as soon as Paul was filled with the Spirit, he immediately reasoned and proved from the Scriptures that Jesus was the Son of God, that the looked-for Messiah was to be the Son of God, and that that man was Jesus.

Yes, the Holy Spirit's witness is a witness to the lordship and deity of the Son of God. Jesus Christ needs no more books written to prove that He is God. He needs no advocate pleading His cause before the unfriendly court of this world. He needs no witness to rise and say, "I know He is the Son of God."

The proof of the Sonship of Jesus has been removed from the realm of the intellect and placed where it has always belonged—in the realm of morals. And it is the Holy Spirit who has put it there. He came, as Jesus had promised, and He is here. He may be grieved and He may have to withdraw from some places, but He is here and He is a silent, holy, eloquent witness.

On Trial Before Him

So, Jesus Christ is no longer on trial before men: but men are now on trial before *Him!*

Strange and wonderful as it may be, He who once stood before Pilate now makes Pilate stand before Him. He who pleaded His cause before the unfriendly world now sits and judges the same world.

He has transferred the religious question to the heart. On the throne He sits, in the form of a Man so we would recognize Him instantly, and He is there invested with full authority and full power and with full right of judgment.

And in our world there is still the holy witness of the Spirit, who in all things speaks for this Man who sits on the throne.

Now, with all my heart I believe in the historicity of the Christian gospel, but that does not mean that the eternal fate of the individual man depends upon historic evidence. The Holy Spirit is here now to convince the world, and however we treat the warning of the Holy Spirit is exactly how we treat Jesus Christ Himself.

If faith must depend upon a man knowing enough of the historical evidences to arrive at a scholarly belief in the deity of Jesus, then there could only be a relatively few people saved. But I do not have to be a scholar, a logician, or a lawyer to arrive at belief in the deity of the Lord Jesus Christ, for the Holy Spirit has taken the deity of Christ out of the hands of the scholars and put it in the consciences of men. The Spirit of God came to lift it out of the history books and write it on the fleshy tablets of the human heart.

I am sure you know that the missionaries go to the jungles where the most primitive men and women cannot read and write. When they proclaim the story of Jesus, when they preach the good news of Jesus Christ as the final answer to sin, the Holy Spirit is faithful in His witness of sin and righteousness and judgment. Those primitive people have never heard of Rome or Greece. They have no idea where Jerusalem is. They never heard of Abraham or David. But when the missionary tells the story of Jesus and the cross and forgiveness of sin, they will begin to tremble and sweat with conviction for they know they are sinners.

When those stone age jungle people put their faith in Jesus Christ as Savior, they are transformed, turned inside out, made good and clean and humble and right. They will learn to read and they will begin to sing songs about the Lord Jesus. They will form themselves into a church. Those great, brawny fellows born in the jungle will become deacons and elders and preachers in that church.

Remember now—they had no knowledge of history, no scholarship, no ability to weigh evidences. They know nothing of relevance or irrelevance; they had never heard of the laws of evidence.

God is able to do His mighty work in His own

way and the Holy Spirit has come into this world
to take polemics away from the scholar and give it
back to the human heart. The believer's faith in the
deity and person of Jesus does not rest upon his
ability to comb through history and arrive at logi-
cal conclusions concerning historic facts. The Holy
Spirit will blaze in on him like a lightning flash,
blinding him with the wonder of it!

That is what Jesus meant when He said, "My
teaching is not my own. It comes from him who
sent me. If anyone chooses to do God's will, he
will find out whether my teaching comes from
God or whether I speak on my own" (7:16-17).

That is why the Holy Spirit has come and that is
why He is here. This is one of the most important
truths that can be taught in the world today. I find
myself wondering about the great majority of
preachers and teachers in Christian circles who
seem so intent upon making the deity of Christ
rest upon historical evidence. I think they must not
discern that the Holy Spirit has taken that matter
completely out of the realm of evidence and has
put it as a burning point in the human conscience.
It is no longer an intellectual problem—it is a
moral problem!

But let's not be too humble and admit that we
are a bunch of dumbbells who barely know our
letters. Augustine had a brilliant mind. Luther was
adept in languages, both in Latin and German.

No, no! You do not have to pump out your head
so that it is a vacuum in order to be a Christian.
We have many ways in which to make use of the

minds God has given us. So keep yours!

However, I repeat: that the use for it will not be in the realm of divine evidences. The Holy Spirit takes care of that.

When our Lord Jesus was here upon the earth all of His ministries to men and women were in dead earnest. When He went into the heavens He sat down in utter and solemn sincerity at the right hand of the Majesty on high. Then the Holy Spirit was sent to us, that wave of silvery light containing in Himself all of the essence of the Father and of the Son. Then as fire He sat upon each of those believers and they had no further question—they knew that Jesus was the Son of God, the Messiah and the Savior. They knew it instantly. They had sensed it before but they did not know for sure. But now they knew!

Confirmation by the Spirit

These are the important things—confirmation by the Spirit of God concerning sin, righteousness, and judgment. The Holy Spirit has not come among us to become involved in a lot of our minor concerns, the trivial things that take up much of our attention.

The Holy Spirit is not here to back you up in your little private quirks and quibbles in prophetic interpretations. The Holy Spirit cannot be used for your arguments about a certain mode of baptism. I have refused to become involved in argument and controversy over the matter of eternal security, because I want the Holy Spirit to help me and guide

me. And He will not help me if I insist on fooling
around in those areas that are not the most important in Christian truth and proclamation.

Now, a lot of people think they are escaping the
conviction of the Spirit by pretending. Many
pretend by saying, "I am a seeker after light."

More often than not, the problem is not a lack of
light. The problem generally turns out to be a
moral problem—but that is how men and women
try to hide and escape—by pretending. Actually,
unbelief is the sign and proof of sin.

On the other hand, saving faith is not a conclusion drawn from facts presented; saving faith is
a gift of God to a penitent man or woman.

There are some frank things that need to be expressed about saving faith in our day, for even in
our evangelical Christian circles there is a basic
misunderstanding of faith.

It is a simple matter to get people to come for-
ward when the invitation is given. It is a simple
matter to get them on their knees. Then what happens?

Someone rushes in with a marked New Testament, sticks a text under their nose, and demands,
"Now, who said that?"

The kneeling person says, "God?"

"Do you believe God?"

"Yes."

"Well, then, do you believe the text?"

"Yes. I must believe it because I believe God."

"Well, then, get right up and testify."

In so many cases, he gets up with an intellectual

faith that has no saving quality.

I continue to oppose that kind of instruction and teaching—the kind that would pick little chickens out of their shells and let them die. I continue to oppose that kind of practice that would take over the work of the Holy Spirit and crowd Him out and retire Him.

This is the age of a superannuated Holy Spirit. We have retired Him and said, "Thanks, we have our Bibles, good King James translation, and we really will not need You until the millennium!"

Others are insisting that it is not the "sin" problem but the "Son" problem that is troubling mankind.

This statement has been credited to a preacher in our day: "Sin has no more meaning to God. On Calvary sin beat itself to death and perished. And now sin has no meaning to God, since Calvary."

He may have been a good man but he was talking like a blooming idiot when he said that. The problem between God and man has always been the sin problem, since that evil hour in the garden. It is true that when the sin question is settled, the Son question comes leaping in—and happily so!

The Holy Spirit deals with us in those three vital areas—sin, righteousness, and judgment.

The Holy Spirit confirms the fact that there has been only one truly holy and righteous man in the world—and He had to leave. They hounded Him out of the world. They said, "This man is not going to make moral fools out of us!" They nailed Him to a cross—and He died for their sins.

Now the Holy Spirit is here to convince the world concerning that unpardoned act, that act of crucifying the world's only truly holy man. For He was holy without being made holy.

There may be holy men now and there may be righteous men now. A man may be righteous now because he has been made righteous by saving faith in the One who never had to be made righteous.

The fact of a coming judgment is ridiculed and ignored by millions who try to shut out the voice of the Spirit. "It is ridiculous to think of God as a bookkeeper or as a file clerk, making little entries and the date of every sin," men have scoffed.

The omniscient God of the universe sees everything perfectly. He knows every person's heartbeat; He knows every thought; He knows every act and every deed. Judgment will not be a difficult thing for the living God. He already knows—and the Holy Spirit is here to convince and confirm.

The Holy Spirit is still among us with transforming power for that one who hears the gospel message and really believes it. The Spirit still raises the consciences of men out of the deep mud of their past. He still converts. He still regenerates. He still transforms. He still makes Christians out of dead clods.

It is tragic that we try to hide from Him in the caves and dens of the earth, among the trees of the garden. It is tragic that men and women keep their hearts so hard that they cannot feel, and so deaf that they cannot hear.

There are many who are hearing the Voice of God, but they insist that the "way" should be made easier for them.

Oh, listen! If hell is what God says it is, if sin is what God says it is, if Jesus Christ had to die to save the sinner—is it asking too much for you to let people know that you are turning from sin?

Jesus Christ never taught that His people would sneak in the easy way. He did not say we could come into the Kingdom of God crawling unobtrusively through the cracks. Never!

If Jesus Christ is your Savior, He has a right to your bold and fearless witness, for He said, "If anyone would come after me, he must deny himself and take up his cross daily and follow me" (Luke 9:23). If you are not willing to do that, you are too big a coward to go to heaven!

The Word of the Lord is not easy but it is safe. Humble yourself and the Lord will draw near to you!

CHAPTER 4

The Blood of Jesus Calls for Mercy and Forgiveness

The LORD said, "What have you done? Listen! Your brother's blood cries out to me from the ground." (Genesis 4:10)

God's revelation to man is very plain, declaring that life is of God and the blood is the symbol of that life. Therefore, our human life is sacred because it is in fact a loan from God Himself. For that reason, the violent crime of shedding another's blood and taking the life is one of the gravest and most destructive sins dealt with in the Scriptures.

The theme of bloodguiltiness is a recurring theme in the Bible and here we have two concepts. The Old Testament picture is that of the blood of murdered Abel crying out for justice. The New Testament picture is that of the blood of Jesus Christ the Savior and mediator crying from the throne of God for mercy!

Must Start with God

We cannot properly consider the voice of Jesus' blood without starting with God Himself, where all true theology begins.

Now, I know that some have said about me: "That man is always talking about God!" I can only say in reply that if that is the only charge that anyone can properly bring against me, I will be quite a happy man. I know that I talk a lot about God—about the triune God—because I still believe in God. I believe in Him as God Almighty, the Father, and Jesus Christ, His Son and our Lord, and the Holy Spirit, the Comforter.

We do begin with God here, where all truth begins, for God is the one true and absolute reality. Back of all, and underneath and supporting all things, He girds the universe and holds it up and guides it.

God does that. That is the only explanation for the universe and the only explanation of human life, for as Creator He gives to human life its meaning and significance.

He is the sacred meaning that gives validity to all meaning. Exclude God from your thinking and you will find yourself with no sense of moral values—you will have no standard of right or wrong. Exclude God from your thinking and good becomes the same as evil and evil is the same as good. Your lie will become truth and truth will be as a lie. Exclude God and it becomes impossible to prove that love is any better than hate. Exclude

God from your thinking and you will not know whether life is any better than death, or whether anything is anything!

So, we begin with God for God is life. All life that exists is God's life. He has given life to all living things and the amazing fact is that God lends life without giving it up!

As humans, we are aware that if we give something away, we give it up for the time it is away from us. But God lends without giving anything up. God gives you life but He is still the life He gives you so He loses nothing by giving it to you.

So with everything else. God is power, but when He gives you power He does not give His power away. He gives wisdom, but He does not lose it when He gives it. He gives grace, but He does not part with His grace. He keeps it while He gives it because it is Himself that He gives.

So it is with everything—wisdom, being, power, holiness and every quality God bestows upon men. God is constantly giving of Himself to us, because God is life!

Life is sacred indeed but we do not fully realize it if we do not believe and confess that it is a gift from God. There is a great truth involved here for human beings—for eternal life can best be described as having God in the soul!

One of the old Puritan fathers gave us that expression: "The life of God in the soul of a man—that is Christianity!" When God gives His life to us He does not give it in the sense of cutting it off from Himself—He knows no diminution of His life or being because He gives us of Himself.

Now, we know the Bible account of how Cain turned on his brother Abel and killed him in a bloody way. We know, too, that Cain's action was not overlooked nor forgotten—for the Lord confronted him with the words, "Listen! Your brother's blood cries out to me from the ground."

In a later time, when David the king was guilty of a number of grievous sins, he had to lay them before his God in confession and prayer. As a man, he was guilty of deception, deceit and disloyalty; he was guilty of adultery and finally of murder.

When David threw himself down to confess and repent, all of these were summed up in his earnest prayer: "Save me from bloodguilt, O God!" (Psalm 51:14).

The compulsion laid upon David, the remorse that brought him to his knees was his own awareness that he was guilty of violating the sacred precincts of life and turning that life out—bloodguiltiness!

Wherever there is bloodguiltiness anywhere in the world you may be sure that society is in trouble.

At this point, some of you may be expecting me to enter into the great modern controversy concerning capital punishment in our society. I do not get involved in the heat of that question. I can only say that I believe the Bible. In the Old Testament it was plain that the only way to deal with bloodguiltiness was to avenge it. The blood of

Abel cried from the ground against the man who had shed that blood.

God wrote into the law of Moses, that if a man shed the blood and took the life of another, he would die for that shedding. The murderer is a presumptuous intruder into the sacred precincts of life. God being life, the murderer in a sense sneaks into the very presence of God and takes that which no man has the right to take except at the hand of God.

Bloodguiltiness lays a great and ruinous burden upon human society, for the voice of blood is the voice of life and the voice of shed blood is the voice of violated life.

I have only the voice and opinion of one man— but I do fear for the future of our great nations on this continent where our laws are taking little account of sin and authorities are letting crime on crime pile up with soft sentiment taking over in so many areas.

There are members of organized crime and killers who boast about their many crimes, and authorities arrest one of the offenders and tell him: "You are a bad boy—you did not pay your income tax!" Meanwhile, the eloquent voice of shed blood cries out to God Almighty!

Shedding of blood has always been a grave sin, because life is in the blood and God gave life to the world, and the nearest thing to life is blood. It follows, then, that the nearest thing to killing God is the killing of the man who was made in the image of God!

I have little fear that any nation or combination of nations could bring down the United States and Canada by military action from without. But this I do fear—we sin and sin and do nothing about it. There is so little sense of the need of repentance— so little burden for the will of God to be wrought in our national life. I fear that the voice of blood will become so eloquent that God Almighty will have no choice but to speak the word that will bring us down.

I do pray often: "Oh God, send a revival of repentance and the fear of God that will sweep through the continent that we may be spared and that we may honor Thee!"

God does hear the eloquence of blood, the eloquence of violated life, and remember that God will always act like Himself—no other way!

God Became Flesh

God became flesh and dwelt among us.

He has said. "What will I do with these bloodstained people? What will I do with the bloodstained world? What will I do with those who have entered into the holy place and shed the blood of men whom I have made in my image?

God said, "I know—I will go myself and become one of them. I will take upon myself the form of a man and I will have blood running in my veins. It will not be the tainted blood of Adam but the pure blood of a second Adam."

So, our Lord came, born of the virgin Mary. There is not a day of my life goes by without my thanks to God for sending His Son, Jesus, made flesh to dwell among us and to die for us.

"He came to that which was his own, but his own did not receive him" (John 1:11).

But He was here and in His veins, I say, there ran that thrice-holy blood of the sinless, untainted Son of Man. Yet, for our sakes, all of the moral corruption of the world, all of the moral pollution of the world was laid on that holy body and charged against that holy soul, for "He made His soul a sacrifice for sin" (see Isaiah 53:10), the Scripture says.

The Savior offered not only His body but His soul as well, for the redemption of mankind. All of the offenses of the human race against God and against each other He bore on that cross—the offenses of Cain against Abel; the offenses of Esau against Jacob; the offenses of David against Uriah; the offenses of Judas in his betrayal of his Lord; the offenses of all of those who killed the martyrs through the centuries; the sins and the offenses of us all!

Oh, I cannot think that we even half believe this!

I think if we even half believed this, it would transform us. It would get into us and possess us so that we could no longer talk about ordinary things. Our minds would run to this wonder so that we could no longer be intent upon everyday matters. We would constantly thank Him and honor Him because in that holy soul and body He bore all of the offenses and pollutions of mankind.

We all reveal the remaining traces of our own

Pharisaism when we point to the Cains and the Neros and the Hitlers and their worst offenses which were laid upon our Lord Jesus Christ, but we were involved at His cross, no matter how quiet and how harmless we seem to be.

One of the great German poets of 200 years ago, von Goethe, summed it up for us all, when he wrote: "I have never heard of a sin being committed without knowing full well that I had the seed of it within myself."

We are on the most blessed ground with our forgiving Savior when we dare to be honest, telling Him, "O dear Lord, I have the potential of all those sins within me. Forgive me and cleanse me and keep me, for Thy glory!"

Yes, the voice of Jesus and the voice of His blood are pleading for us, and remember this: The voice of Jesus is not the voice of a murdered man.

The Holy Spirit through the Apostle Peter charged that generation of Jesus' day with these words: "You men of Israel have taken Him, a man approved of God among you, and by wicked hands have crucified and slain Him" (see Acts 2:22-23).

It was not a murder they committed, although they meant it to be so. It was a Sacrifice offered, God turning a cross into an altar and the condemned one into a Lamb. It was a Man offering Himself on an altar of sacrifice, not a man dying on the cross for his sin. He was the only Man who had no sins for which to die. He died and shed His blood for violated blood.

I have said I fear for human society today, piling up blood on violated blood, but I also find this hope coming to my heart. I remember that in the blood of Christ the blood of the world was shed. Sometimes we sing

> Bread of the world in mercy broken
> wine of the soul in mercy shed;
> By whom the words of life were spoken,
> and in whose death our sins are dead.

Paul was speaking for us when he said, "For Christ's love compels us, because we are convinced that one died for all, and therefore all died. And he died for all, that those who live should no longer live for themselves but for him who died for them and was raised again" (2 Corinthians 5:14-15).

So, Christ's blood was our blood—and this is the theology of New Testament victory for the believer. This is the theology that I experienced as a young man in The Christian and Missionary Alliance.

This is the theology that tells me that Christ and I are united, so that when He died I died, and when He arose I arose! This is the doctrine of spiritual victory and there is no other way that consistent victory can be found.

Spiritual victory comes only by the knowledge that we died.

I must die! I must die!

It is not true, as some seem to think, that God can

make a transfer and say: "Well, I will let this Man die in your stead and you will just go free and get out of it!" That is not quite the way God has done it.

What He did was to join me to that Man, Jesus Christ, by the wonder and mystery of incarnation on His part, and regeneration in us. He joined us to that man so that when He died, we died. It was not only a transfer, it was not only a vicarious act—it was an actuality!

Dead in Christ

The Scriptures say that every Christian believer may consider himself to have died in Christ. Give yourselves over for a time to the study of chapters 5 through 8 in the book of Romans. You will see for yourself that this is the doctrine of the Bible: that when Christ became humanity, He made it possible for us to get up into deity—not to become deity but to be united with deity.

God counts Christ's death to be my death and He counts the sacrifice Christ laid down to be mine.

I repeat: "For Christ's love compels us, because we are convinced that one died for all, and therefore all died. . . . that those who live should no longer live for themselves" (5:14-15).

No man has any right to sin again now—the voice of Jesus' blood is eloquent now, one of the most eloquent sounds in the human mind.

Wherever you find Christ's church, wherever her songs are raised, wherever the prayers of her saints rise we hear the voice of Jesus' blood pleading eloquently, and witnessing that "in the blood of Christ the sins of the world died" (see 1 John 2:2).

Oh, if men and women will only believe it!

When will we realize and confess that every sin is now a moral incongruity? As believers, we are supposed to have died with Jesus Christ our Lord. When we were joined to Him in the new birth we were joined to His death. When we were joined to His rising again, it should have been plain to us that sin is now a moral incongruity in the life of a Christian.

The sinner sins because he is out there in the world—and he has never died. He is waiting to die and he will die once and later he will die the second death.

But a Christian dies with Christ and dies in Christ and dies along with Christ, so that when he lays his body down at last the Bible says he will not see death.

God will cover the eyes of all Christians when the time comes—they never see death. The Christian stops breathing and there is a burial but he does not see death—for he already died in Christ when Christ died, and he arose with Christ when Christ arose.

That is why sin is a moral incongruity in the life and deportment of the Christian believer. It is a doctrine and theology completely unknown to those whose Christianity is like a button or flower stuck on the lapel—completely external.

I believe the gospel of Jesus Christ saved me completely—therefore He asks me for total commitment. He expects me to be a disciple totally dedicated.

Joined to Jesus Christ, how can we be other than what He is? What He does, we do. Where He leads, we go. This is genuine Christianity!

Sin is now an outrage against holy blood. To sin now is to crucify the Son of God afresh. To sin now is to belittle the blood of atonement. For a Christian to sin now is to insult the holy life laid down. I cannot believe that any Christian wants to sin.

All offenses against God will either be forgiven or avenged—we can take our choice. All offenses against God, against ourselves, against humanity, against human life—all offenses will be either forgiven or avenged. There are two voices—one pleading for vengeance, the other pleading for mercy.

What a terrible thing for men and women to get old and have no prospect, no gracious promise for the long eternity before them.

But how beautiful to come up like a ripe shock of corn and know that the Father's house is open, the doors are wide open and the Father waits to receive His children one after another!

Some years ago one of our national Christian brothers from the land of Thailand gave his testimony in my hearing. He told what it had meant in his life and for his future when the missionaries came with the good news of the gospel of Christ.

He described the godly life of one of the early missionaries and then said: "He is in the Father's house now."

He told of one of the missionary women and the love of Christ she had displayed, and then said: "She is in the Father's house now."

What a vision for a humble Christian who only a generation before had been a pagan, worshiping idols and spirits—and now because of grace and mercy he talks about the Father's house as though it were just a step away, across the street.

This is the gospel of Christ—the kind of Christianity I believe in. What joy to discover that God is not mad at us and that we are His children—because Jesus died for us, because the blood of Jesus "speaks a better word than the blood of Abel" (Hebrews 12:24). What a blessing to find out that the mercy of God speaks louder than the voice of justice. What a hope that makes it possible for the Lord's people to lie down quietly when the time comes and whisper, "Father, I am coming home!"

Oh, we ought to make more of the blood of the Lamb, because it is by the blood that we are saved; by the blood atonement is made.

You know I encourage you to sing some of the old camp meeting songs with plain theology and clear message. This is one of those:

The cross, the cross, the bloodstained cross,
The hallowed cross I see;

Reminding me of precious blood
That once was shed for me.

A thousand, thousand fountains spring
Up from the throne of God;
But none to me such blessings bring
As Jesus' precious blood.

That priceless blood my ransom paid
When I in bondage stood;
On Jesus all my sins were laid,
He saved me with His blood.

By faith that blood now sweeps away
My sins, as like a flood;
Nor lets one guilty blemish stay;
All praise to Jesus' blood!

This wondrous theme will best employ
My heart before my God;
And make all heaven resound with joy
For Jesus' cleansing blood.

The blood of Jesus Christ continues to plead eloquently. At the right hand of God the Father I do
not believe that Jesus, our great high priest, has to
talk and talk. I am sure His intercession for us lies
in His two wounded hands.

When children of God violate the covenant, God
hears the voice of the wounded Son of God and
forgives, but is that reason for us to be careless?
Never! Never while the world stands!

We Christians ought to be the cleanest, purest, most righteous, holiest people in all the world—for the blood of Jesus Christ can sweep away our sins "as like a flood, [not let] one guilty blemish stay; all praise to Jesus' blood!"

CHAPTER 5

The Ground of Human Conscience: Christ's Presence in the World

So when they continued asking him, he lifted up himself, and said unto them, He that is without sin among you, let him first cast a stone at her. And again he stooped down, and wrote on the ground. And they which heard it,being convicted by their own conscience, went out one by one, beginning at the eldest, even unto the last. . . . (John 8:7-9, KJV)

The enemy of our souls has long been using a subtle, pseudo-learned type of propaganda to bring derision and disrepute to man of life's verities—and among these is conscience. When human conscience is mentioned in learned circles in our day, it is mentioned only with a smirk.

If it is to be considered seriously, it is necessary

that we must defend the whole concept of human conscience. That seems almost unbelievable—but it is true!

Personally, I cannot ignore that which the universal wisdom of the human race in all ages has approved—the idea of a moral conscience within the being of every man.

Neither do I feel that I must defend that which the Christian Scriptures take for granted and consistently teach throughout. If you will trace it through your concordance you will find that conscience is mentioned in many, many places. Beyond that, the idea which the word "conscience" embodies appears throughout the Bible, as though woven into its very fabric.

We should first explore what we mean by conscience; then point to this Bible example to see it in operation, and finally, show that it is a voice still calling to mankind.

A Moral Awareness

I think it must be said of conscience that it is a moral awareness; that it always deals with right and wrong and the relationship of the individual to right and wrong. Conscience never deals with theories about anything.

You will also note a strange thing in the Bible record: conscience always deals in the singular, never in the plural, as in this instance: "they . . . being convicted by their own conscience, went out."

It is always true in the Bible that conscience refers to right and wrong, and is individual and personal and singular. Conscience never lets you lean on someone else. Conscience singles you out of the crowd as though no one else exists.

John does not record that the scribes and Pharisees departed in a group when Jesus said, "Let him that is without sin cast the first stone." They went out one by one. Each went out driven by his own conscience.

In this sense, the word conscience means a moral sight. It means to see completely. It means a secret, inward awareness, and I think we would call that the psychological definition of conscience. But that is not our concern in this lesson. We want to study and learn something more about the ground of human conscience—and I believe that the ground of human conscience is the secret presence of Christ in the world.

That explains why conscience is a moral awareness!

This brings me to a verse that is very basic in my theology: "That was the true Light, which lighteth every man that cometh into the world" (1:9, KJV).

Jesus is that light that is in the world, and His secret presence lights every man that comes into the world.

That is the ground of moral conscience. However it operates, that is the ground. That is how men and women in this world have a secret awareness of moral values.

There are some Bible teachers who insist that when the Bible says that we are dead in trespasses and sins it means we are dead in a very literal sense of the word. Their teaching is this: the sinner, being dead, has no moral awareness at all.

I think that kind of excgesis is so bad and so confused that it has no place at all in considering the Scriptures. I do not think you can make the Bible say that a man who is dead in sin is a completely dead man—one who can neither be persuaded nor convinced, pleaded with nor appealed to, convicted nor frightened. Who can say that the person who has not yet come to Christ is just a dead lump?

Being dead in our sin means that we are cut off from the life of God—and that is so bad that it is impossible to think of anything worse. But that man who is dead in sin, cut off from the life of God, does have a moral awareness. He does hear a secret inner voice. The light that lights every man that comes into the world—that is the singular voice in the bosom of every human being, accusing or else excusing him, as the Apostle Paul said.

That is what I mean by conscience.

In the eighth chapter of John, we have a striking Bible example of the conscience in operation.

The scribes and Pharisees insisted that they were strict moralists, and they appeared to be when anyone was watching. They wanted to silence Jesus and to discredit His teachings, so they dragged a miserable woman into His presence and said, "Teacher, this woman was caught in the act of adultery. In the Law Moses commands us to stone such women. Now what do you say?" (8:4-5).

Jesus looked at the accusing men and he knew

everything that was in their hearts. He knew they had no concern at all for the wretched woman. He knew that their concern was not at all for the broken law. He knew they had no thought for the religion nor for the society of Israel.

He knew they only had one thing in mind—discrediting Him forever. He knew the woman was only a pawn in their plan. They had no love for her and they really had no hatred for her sin. But they hated Jesus and they would do anything to get at Him.

They thought they had an open-and-shut case. If Jesus said, "Stone her to death," and they did, the Roman rulers would immediately throw Jesus into prison and that would be the end of Him.

If Jesus said, "Let her go," they could make their case against Him: "We always knew you were against the Law of Moses!" If they could discredit His teachings concerning the Law of Moses that would be the end of Him in Israel.

Jesus was well aware of their hatred, of their hypocrisy and of the kind of frame-up they had rigged. He had no regard for their outward pretensions of praying in public to be seen and heard, for their sanctimonious appearance, or for their pious nasal breathing.

But they were anxious for Jesus to speak. They believed the trap was all set.

I think Jesus looked every one of them directly in the eye during that moment—and I have to believe that there was a twinkle in the heart, if not in the eye of Jesus.

First he stooped down and with His finger wrote something in the dust of the ground.

John records that they were anxious and impatient, for they continued pressing Him, asking Him to answer.

Jesus said simply, "Fellows, let the one of you who has never sinned cast the first stone at her."

In his record, John says, "being convicted by their own conscience, they went out one by one" (8:9, KJV).

Each of those accusing men slipped out quietly by himself—each ashamed to say anything to the others. Each one alone—because it is in the power of conscience to isolate the human soul and take away all of its hopes and helps and encouragements.

Some of those seemingly pious religionists had thought that because they were old and had forgotten their early sins, that God had forgotten them, also. But as soon as the voice of Jesus roused them within, they remembered and they sneaked out, afraid to look up for fear God would start throwing stones at them.

Actually, the Mosaic law of stoning never was intended to mean that a wicked man could stone a wicked woman. It never had the intent that one sinner could put another sinner to death—and Jesus knew that.

Pardon me if my language is plain but it occurs to me that when those old hypocrites ran up against Jesus, it was like a cat running into a mowing machine. When they came away, each one was licking his wounds of conviction and conscience.

That is how this business of conscience works. It smites the inner life. It touches the heart. It isolates the individual. It sets us off all by ourselves.

That is the terror of the conscience and I think it will be the cosmic loneliness of the lost soul before an angry God that will put the hell in judgment.

Now, I am wondering what has happened that Christians no longer really believe in the human conscience.

The fact of conscience has been laughed out of court, pushed aside by the propaganda of hell, so that even churches are afraid to admit to conscience.

But the Bible stands firm—it is not afraid to admit the truth of conscience.

The Bible says bluntly: "Being convicted by their own conscience, they went out one by one." Those men were conscience-stricken, smitten inside, struck as if by a stroke from heaven. They had to get out of there in order to sneak away.

An Inner Voice

Conscience is that inner voice that keeps speaking within our beings—and it deserves something better from us than wisecracks and humor.

We should all be aware by this time that one way the devil has of getting rid of something is to make jokes about it. Every one of us needs to be warned often about the corruption of our minds by the papers and magazines and entertainment.

There is a legitimate humor, and we all admit that. I think a sense of humor is in us by the gift of God.

But whenever that humor takes a holy thing as its object, that humor is devilish at once. One of the sick jokes you have heard insists that conscience is that part of you that makes you sorry when you get caught. That is supposed to be funny but it is not. It is tragic that so many have yielded so far to the propaganda of hell as to joke about that which is no joke.

I respect the integrity of Emerson, that old New Englander, who would never allow anyone to joke about love or death in his presence. We ought to agree with him that there are some things that are not proper objects of humor.

One of these is conscience, the power that God has set in the human breast, able to isolate a soul and to hang it between heaven and hell, as lonely as if God had never created another soul. The light that lights every man who comes into the world is not a joking matter.

The eternal, universal light-giving presence of Christ is not a joking matter. These things are all too serious to be dealt with lightly.

There is plenty to laugh at in the world, including politics—which is usually funny anyway. But be sure that you do not laugh at something that God Himself takes very seriously. Remember that conscience is always on God's side—always on God's side. It judges conduct in the light of the moral law, and as the Scriptures say, it either excuses or accuses.

It is not too much to say that every one of us, every one who has come into the world, has heard a voice from God in our own time equal to the voice of Jesus when He was here on earth.

I say that because many people seem to think they are cheated: "Oh, if only I could have heard A.B. Simpson or Dwight Moody."

You have heard the first voice and the last voice. You have heard the voice of the inner conscience. You have known a moral illumination because of the One who by His presence lights every man. Do you know that there were tens of thousands who heard Jesus when He was on earth and had no idea what He was talking about?

Do you know that some of His own disciples had to wait for the Holy Spirit at Pentecost to know and understand what Jesus had been telling them?

Jesus had to assure his own disciples, "It is for your good that I am going away" (16:7).

Returning to that long-past day is not the answer to the need of the believers in the Christian church today. God is certainly dealing with many who need to give heed and listen to the inner voice, and then do something about it!

Harming the Conscience

The Bible tells us several things that men may do to their conscience.

Timothy wrote that "The goal of this command is love which comes from a pure heart and a good conscience and a sincere faith. Some have wandered away from these and turned to meaningless talk" (1 Timothy 1:5-6).

Some people have turned away from a good conscience. They will be found among the Christians who live carelessly. All the sermons in the world will be wasted if there is not a good, clean conscience to receive the truth.

Timothy also wrote by the Spirit about those "hypocritical liars whose consciences have been seared as with a hot iron" (4:2).

We often see that those men and women with a seared conscience will be led into false doctrines.

We wonder how it is possible for a man who has been in the fellowship of the Word of truth to turn away suddenly into some false religion.

Perhaps his friends will say that his mind was confused but we should be honest about this—for false doctrines can have no power upon a good conscience. But when a conscience has become seared, when a man has played with the fire and burned his conscience and calloused it until he can handle the hot iron of sin without shrinking, there is no longer any safety for him.

Titus wrote in his epistle about those to whom nothing is pure any longer, "both their minds and consciences are corrupted" (Titus 1:15).

Here Titus speaks of an inward corruption, revealed in impure thoughts and soiled language. I am just as afraid of people with soiled tongues as I am of those with a communicable disease.

Actually, a foul tongue is an evidence of a deeper

spiritual disease and Titus goes on to tell us that those with defiled conscience become reprobates, something just washed up on the shore, a moral shipwreck.

What a relief to find the writer to the Hebrews encouraging us to "draw near to God with a sincere heart in full assurance of faith, having our hearts sprinkled to cleanse us from a guilty conscience" (Hebrews 10:22).

A sprinkled conscience—surely this is a gracious thing for men and women in the world to know!

One of the most relieving, enriching, wholesome, wondrous things we can know is that sudden sense of the lifting of the burden as the conscience goes free—God giving freedom to that conscience which has been evil, diseased and protesting.

Peter wrote about this and called it "the pledge of a good conscience toward God. It saves you by the resurrection of Jesus Christ" (1 Peter 3:21).

This is the kind of conversion I believe in—when your sins are cleansed and forgiven through the blood of the Lamb, you will know it!

You can take your sins and your evil conscience to a priest and he will give you absolution. But he is only able to bury your conscience under a little religious rag and if ever you get right with God, it will come right back at you.

Oh, there is an inner voice either accusing or excusing, and when you have had the answer of a good conscience, you can get up and know it is all right. A transaction has taken place within the human spirit. The heart suddenly knows itself clean and the burden lifts from the mind and there is a true sense that heaven is pleased and God is smiling and the sins are gone.

A transaction within the human spirit—that is the kind of forgiveness I believe in!

I once slipped into a noonday service in New York City and I heard something I will never be able to forget.

A minister speaking that day said: "We assume that if a man has heard the Christian gospel he has been enlightened. But that is a false assumption. Just to have heard a man preach truth from the Bible does not necessarily mean that you have been enlightened."

God's voice must speak from within to bring enlightenment. It must be the Spirit of God speaking soundlessly within—that is what brings him in and makes him accountable to God. Just the words of a text falling upon a human ear may not mean anything.

Many years ago, the godly Horatious Bonar wrote: "A seared conscience is the sinner's heritage. It is upon this that the Holy Spirit first lays His hand when He awakens the soul from its sleep of death. He touches the conscience, and then the struggles of conviction come. He then pacifies it by the sprinkling of the blood, showing it Jesus and His cross. Then giving it the taste of forgiveness, it rests from all its tumults and fears."

I believe that God has related these somehow: the voice of conviction in the conscience and the

Holy Spirit, the point of contact, witnessing within man's being. A person has not been illuminated until that voice begins to sound within him.

Men and women need to be told that it may be fatal to silence the inner voice. It is always perilous to resist the conscience within; but it may be fatal to silence that voice, to continue to ignore that speaking voice within!

CHAPTER
6

The Christian Is a Realist: He Sees Things as They Are

Wash and make yourselves clean.
Take your evil deeds
  out of my sight!
Stop doing wrong,
  learn to do right!
Seek justice,
  encourage the oppressed.
Defend the cause of the fatherless,
  plead the case of the widow.

"Come now, let us reason together,"
  says the LORD.
"Though your sins are like scarlet,
  they shall be as white as snow;
though they are red as crimson,
  they shall be like wool.
If you are willing and obedient,
  you will eat the best from the land."
    (Isaiah 1:16-19)

People with many different insights have given us a variety of definitions for the word "reason." The dictionary says reason has to do with comprehension and inference, with a sound mind; with motive and judgment; and with the ground of reality which makes a fact intelligible.

I have thought a good deal about reason and I have come up with a brief sentence which I think may express it well for us: Reason is a wise recognition of things as they really are.

If this is true, then Christian believers are the most reasonable of all persons—and the true realists.

If this is true, then Christians are not the dreamers, after all! They are truly realists because they insist on stripping things down to their hard core of reality. Scientists boast that they test everything and pull it down to its reality. But the genuine Christian is a sounder, truer realist than a scientist can ever be, for the Christian insists upon knowing what really is true.

The Christian wants to know what is true about life—the scientist wants to know what is true about life, but by logic.

The Christian wants to know what is true about life in its broad and everlasting relationships. The Christian wants to know about his sins—where they are and what happened to them. He wants to know about God and judgment and his own relationship to God and to immortality and eternal life.

His insistence upon knowing is according to reason, for reason is a wise recognition of things as they really are—not as they seem to be.

The Great Pretender

I must charge it back upon the worldling, the unsaved man, that he is really the unrealistic person because he must spend his whole life pretending. If I were to invent a title to cover the *genus homo*, the human being, unsaved and out of Christ, I would have to call him "the great pretender."

For instance, he must pretend all of his lifetime that he is not going to die. He must put on that act day after day, month after month. That is not realism—it is the fuzziest kind of fantasy in which humans can indulge.

What is it with us?—humans continually acting in a pretense that we are never going to die yet knowing all the time that we must and that we will!

But the Christian has become a realist.

He is already prepared for the next chapter. He has packed his suitcase, and he is ready to go. In fact, you may see him somewhere sitting on his suitcase, with the pair of steel rails close by. He knows for a certainty that the train is on the way and that it is not going to pass him by. He is the realist, and it is the other fellow who is the dreamer of deadly and fateful dreams.

Throughout his lifetime, the sinner is forced to close his eyes and pretend not to see. He is forced to cover up and hide and dodge and twist and put on another face. When he hears that his friend has dropped dead on the golf course, he swallows his Adam's apple and takes refuge in his masculine vocal chords and says: "Too bad."

He was scared stiff when he heard it because he thought that he might be next.

That man is not a realist. He is a hypocrite and a pretender and a liar—and he is forced to go through life in that way.

It is the Christian believer who deals with things as they are. The Christian is not on the defensive. It is actually the worldling, the unbeliever, who is on the defensive during his entire lifetime.

I believe it is entirely proper and fitting for the Christian church to be on the offensive. I believe that we should be reminding the world that the Christian man and the Christian woman are the true realists—that we have gone through and settled some everlasting facts.

The Christian message is according to reason: "Come now, let us reason together" (1:18).

The Christian message takes into account God and man and man's relation to God. It takes into account sin and man's relation to sin and responsibility for sin and accountability to God under that responsibility. It takes into account judgment and death, the shortness of life, and the deceitfulness of appearances.

The genuine Christian is one whose house is always in order. He does not have to stampede and implore heaven in panic when he finds he is going to die. He has only a few legal matters to settle, for as far as his everlasting relationships are concerned he has already realistically taken care of them. To him, the Christian message is according to reason.

Now, God being who He is and what He is, there is in the Godhead and in man's relationship to God a transcendency that outstrips reason. But also, it must be said, there is never anything in that relationship that outrages reason.

On the Offensive

It is from this position that we ought to be on the offensive for our Christian faith!

We ought to confront the sinner, with all of his learning, and insist that while our faith and assurance transcend reason, they never outrage it. We are not unreasonable in our belief—we are just men and women who live according to the highest reason there is. The Christian message is reasonable and altogether according to the facts, and according to the sound judgment and recognition of things as they really are!

Now, if you have done any serious reading you have no doubt discovered the charge made by some critics that reason says one thing and religion says something else.

I dare to say that whoever says that is still wet behind his intellectual ears, for religion is on the side of reason, always. Whatever is irreligious and unbelieving is on the side of unreason and not on the side of reason.

Consider the fact that when our Lord Jesus

Christ calls to men His entreaty is based upon reasonable considerations. One of these is certainly our lost condition. That is a reasonable consideration.

The devil has had a lot of success with his propaganda so that many people no longer accept the Bible doctrine that men are lost.

The argument seems to be: "We are not lost. We are on our way upward. We are still struggling upward!"

No one can fool me with this "struggling upward" business. Man has been struggling for a long, long time and he is no nearer to being "up" than he ever was.

When we are realistic we confess that we are a lost people. We are still quite young when we begin to notice that our physical frame is susceptible to many ills—because we belong to a lost and dying race.

Why do we have wars and rumors of wars? Why do we have political corruption and dictatorships and slavery and bondage of many kinds? Why do we have police on every corner and why do we have jails and prisons and insane asylums?

Because we humans are a lost people—and it is a lost world in which we live. Anyone who refuses to consider the symptoms is completely unrealistic.

It is the Christian message that takes man's lost condition frankly into account and refuses to listen to the propaganda of unreason that says we are not lost.

Actually, the lostness of man is not a dogma—it

is a fact. We are not dealing in the realm of fancy. We are dealing with facts as hard and realistic as a brick that goes into the solid construction of a building.

So, the Christian says, "Men are lost and we know they are lost."

The Christian message is based upon reason. It is based on the redeeming work of Christ which is made necessary by the lost condition of mankind. It is based upon the love of God in Christ Jesus and it is based upon the power of the gospel. It is based upon the fact that humanity is perishing. It is based upon the abiding permanence of the will of God, and it is based upon the importance of immediate action!

The Christian message is based upon all of these sound, realistic facts, so it is the unbeliever who is put on the defensive. He is the one who must be able to give a reason for what lies within his being. The Christian knows—and he has confessed his need and confessed his Savior and is ready for the next chapter.

Notice that in the text there is the stern voice of exhortation as well as the gracious voice of promise.

These are joined, as a poet has said, "in reason's ear."

We do listen to the stern voice of God's exhortation: "Wash and make yourselves clean. Take your evil deeds out of my sight! Stop doing wrong, learn to do right! Seek justice, encourage the oppressed. Defend the cause of the fatherless, plead the case of the widow" (1:16-17).

"Come now, let us reason together," the Lord is saying to us. "Though your sins are like scarlet, they shall be as white as snow; though they are red as crimson, they shall be like wool" (1:18).

Surely that is the gracious voice of promise.

Will you believe me when I say that we do a great injury to mankind when we divide these two voices—exhortation and promise? We have no excuse for insisting that we make a solo out of that which God meant to be a duet.

Two Sides of a Coin

God meant this message to be two sides of the same coin—but we split the coin edgewise and in a sense ruin both sides.

The illustration holds, for it takes both sides of a half dollar coin to be worth fifty cents. Get a fine saw and split it edgewise and neither side will buy you a one-cent stamp.

Many get into the Bible and become adept in the art of splitting texts edgewise and destroying both.

I go to my Bible and I read: "Wash and make yourselves clean. Take your evil deeds out of my sight! Stop doing wrong, learn to do right" (1:16-17). If I stop there I am splitting the coin edgewise and it is of no value.

If I go to my Bible and I skip the first part and only read: "Come, let us reason together. . . . Though your sins are like scarlet, they shall be as white as snow" (1:18), and read nothing before or nothing after, I have split the coin edgewise and it has no value either. Yet we have whole schools of Christian theology based upon such splitting, texts ripped apart and divided asunder.

In this portion, the voices are here as a duet. God is sovereign and reason is singing her two songs— the stern voice of exhortation and the gracious voice of promise!

We can do great soul injury to men and women by trying to indicate that we can have our sins forgiven, washed and cleansed, without first turning from evil and putting it away from before God's eyes; ceasing to do evil, learning to do good.

The teaching of forgiveness without any turning from sin is a great error and it has filled the churches with deceived members and helped to fill hell with deceived souls.

It cannot be denied that many people have come into the church on a half-text. "Though your sins are like scarlet, they shall be as white as snow"— they forget that that is only half the text.

Neither can it be denied that there are some who are driven away from the churches because of the preaching of only the first half of the text—"Wash and make yourselves clean!"

They stand back and say, "Dear God, how can I? How can a man as vile as I am ever wash me? Even if I had all the acids in the world I could not cleanse my soul!" Such as these go away discouraged—because they hear the emphasis on only half the text.

This matter is a grave error, because the teaching

and the hope of being forgiven while persisting in sin is a great moral impossibility. It does violence to the Scriptures and it also violates moral reason.

The voice of moral reason insists that all pardon is conditioned upon intention to reform, and I realize here that some people will not allow the use of the word "reform."

I have heard people condemn this word reform. They stand straight and click their heels together and declare: "I do not believe in reformation; I believe only in regeneration."

I could very well say to them: "I do not believe in the 'In God We Trust' side of the coin—only the 'E Pluribus Unum' side."

Both sides are there. They are necessary to give any value to the coin, and let me tell you that reformation and regeneration are not enemies! They are friends. I could say they are Siamese twins, for forgiveness is based upon the intention to reform.

Actually, reform is another word for repent. Do your first works. Clean up. Get right. Straighten out.

A story has been told about a governor of one of the states. He was concerned about the plight of many in the prison system, and he visited one of the prisons, going incognito. The prisoners did not know who he was.

Having opportunity to talk to a young man, he asked why he was there and for how long.

"I suppose you would like to get outside again," the governor said in conversation.

"I would sure like to be out," was the reply. "but I doubt it. They threw the book at me."

Then the governor asked: "Tell me, if you were free again, what would be the first thing you would do?"

The face of the inmate changed to a grim scowl and he almost growled as he said: "The first thing I would do would be to cut the throat of that blankety-blank judge that sent me here!"

The governor, the man with the power to pardon and release, had not expected to hear that kind of snarl. He was hoping for an indication of remorse and repentance and reform. He was hoping he might hear a prisoner's desire to be a good man again, desiring to try and straighten out the wrongs that had put him in that place.

He stayed in there, you see, because pardons are conditioned upon intention to reform. You cannot save a man who insists upon continuing in the things that cause him to be unsaved.

A lifeguard can pluck a drowning man out of the water but what can he do if the man turns right back and throws himself into the water again? A fireman can carry a person out of a flaming, settling building but what can he do if the person runs right back into the fire?

In the spiritual and moral realm, then, it is a glaring inconsistency to try to teach forgiveness where there is no intention to reform. To teach pardon and cleansing where there is no intention to change the life would upset heaven and turn it into a moral insane asylum, and in a hundred years you would not know heaven from hell!

Another thing to mention here is that intention can be proved only by the changed and transformed life. That is the only way of knowing.

Notice that in the text we have taken there are nine active verbs. Wash, make, take, stop, learn, seek, encourage, defend, plead—nine active verbs.

Perhaps you recall your English class and the difference between the passive voice and the active voice.

When the passive voice is used the subject receives the action. I just stand here and someone does something to me. I passively receive the act.

But, if I do something, that is the active voice. If I say, "I am loved," that is passive. Someone loves me, I receive the action. I do not have to do a thing but stand here and look pretty.

But, if I say, "I love someone," that is active voice. That is positive.

This brings me right to the point that the curse of religion today is that we are completely in the passive voice. We are on the receiving end of everything. We want everything coming our way.

God has said, "Though your sins are like scarlet, they shall be as white as snow." But God saw fit to put nine active verbs ahead of that word.

We say, "I am washed." That is the passive voice.

The Lord says, "Wash! Take your evil deeds out of my sight!"

Our danger in spiritual matters is that everything is done for us and everything is done to us. We are spectators instead of being participants.

The Lord has spoken to us all and said, "If you are willing and obedient, you will eat the best from the land" (1:19).

Willing and obedient Christians—where are they? Why do we have so many spineless and shrinking Christians, apparently without any strength of character?

Why should we find a Christian man praying, "Oh Lord, help me to be honest." He knows well enough that if he is not honest he will go to jail.

I have heard people pray, "Oh Father, help me to quit lying." God never taught them to lie—He just says, "Quit your lying."

Many Christians seem to go through life unable to resist temptation, unable to wage the warfare of prayer, unwilling to suffer for Jesus' sake.

Our Lord Jesus Christ asked us to be His witnesses and to stand firm in the faith. Instead, many of us settle for being a kind of religious jellyfish.

It is time that we Christians wake up and assume our spiritual responsibilities. Let us ask God to wind up our backbones; let us ask Him to give us the courage to pray. "Now, God, show me what to do!" and get out there and get active.

If we "are willing and obedient, [we] will eat the best from the land"—that is the promise of God. But if we refuse and rebel, nothing but judgment lies before us.

God is calling us and we have every sound reason why we should follow Him faithfully. There is every sound reason why we should be committed, out-and-out Christians; and not one lonely reasonable argument for staying unsaved or staying half-saved.

Every voice of reason cries out for us not only to consider God's gracious plan of salvation, but for us to totally yield and obey—"for then will I cleanse you whiter than snow and make you as white as wool."

The Eternal Worth of the Soul: God Calls—"Be Ye Reconciled"

But God said to him, "You fool! This very night your life will be demanded from you." (Luke 12:20)

It is declared in the Bible, as well as being often assumed, that man has a conscious and living soul.

Our Lord Jesus Christ in His teachings took it for granted that men and women know they have souls. You cannot find a passage anywhere in the New Testament where Jesus said, in so many words: "Verily, I say unto you, man has a soul." He did not need to say it.

The fact that man is a being with a living soul was then, and is now, a common coin of knowledge. It is taken for granted in the Bible just as we take the dollar for granted in our monetary system. A department store does not have to put up big signs on every floor saying: "Remember the dollar is worth ten dimes, four quarters, twenty nickels."

We all take that for granted—it is a common coin, the common unit of value.

So, the Bible takes the fact of the soul of man for granted. It does not have to everlastingly assert it.

Now, consider this fact. If the government should devaluate the dollar to zero, we would have no monetary system remaining in the United States.

Likewise, if you take away the truth that a man has a soul, you devaluate the man. You reduce him to something less than a man, for God in creation breathed the breath of life into man, and he became a living soul.

Now, to some, it might seem like putting up a paper tiger to slay to make the insistence that man has a soul. I have long claimed that much in fundamental circles is the solemn repetition of an undisputed thing, and I do not want to fall into that snare. But on the other hand, I know the age in which I live. I am sure that this is the hour when the soul of man is getting less attention than it has since the beginning and rise of revealed religion.

The Worth of the Soul

The eternal worth of the soul needs again to be declared as having worth over against all other human values. There is nothing else that can be compared with the human soul.

Actually, the Bible not only weaves the truth of

man's soul in and out throughout the fabric of theology as a golden thread, but it also declares it as a hard tenet of truth.

The truth of the reality of the soul has been accepted and believed by all people and all races and all religions since time began. There are differences in the concepts, but most people throughout the ages have accepted the fact that there is an essential something that lives within the inner nature of man and that the outward, physical body is only the tabernacle in which the living soul dwells.

One may almost say that the belief in the fact of the human soul is a test of our humanity.

Every once in a while we hear of some rare pigheaded individual who insists that man does not have a soul. It is interesting to me that such individuals generally turn out to be strange and extreme persons. They become suspect and are usually looked upon as something of a monster in society.

Actually, what has he done? He has dehumanized himself and sold out the value of himself as a human being. He has insisted on being something less than a man.

If such a man leads his dog down the street and stops and talks to a friend, saying, "I do not believe in the soul," he not only dehumanizes himself but he makes himself less than the dog by his side.

If the man does not have a soul, then his dog is better off than he is. The dog can survive under worse conditions. The dog can get along with less food than the man. The dog does not live under the weight of many human responsibilities. The dog pays no taxes and does not worry at all about the future and death and the judgment.

We read in the Scripture about the souls of the righteous being in the hands of God. The psalmist in the Old Testament admonishes us to be still and talk to our own soul as he did while lying on his bed.

When Jesus spoke of the soul in His time, He was speaking about that part of man's being which is endless, which lives on and on. He certainly was not speaking of the physical body in which man lives.

The Body Is Amoral

The body is mere matter, and as the Bible says, fades as a leaf. When we are about sixteen, we are prone to think that our strong, healthy bodies will last forever. When we are about twice sixteen, we begin to worry a little about the body. When we are about four times sixteen, we are willing to admit the truth—the physical body has no continuing life of its own.

For that reason I can never get mad at the human body as some people do, blaming the body for everything. Read the Bible and you will find it never blames the human body for anything: it is only the tabernacle in which the human being lives.

The body is completely amoral—it is neither good nor bad. It has no moral quality attached to it. It is simply a dwelling place.

A man buys an automobile and gets behind the

wheel and with purpose drives over someone he does not like and kills him. Do we blame the automobile and hold it responsible?

Of course we do not. The automobile as an object is completely amoral. It is the man who gets behind the wheel and guides it who for the moment gives some moral quality to it.

The fact that a good man drives an automobile and guides it so that it takes him to church to worship is a good thing. The same automobile might be driven by an evil man taking him to his companions in a gambling den—but the car itself is neither good nor bad. It is the man who is driving the car who makes it what he wants it to be for the moment.

So with the human body. It is the humble and helpless servant of the man who lives within it.

You live in that body of yours, and you cannot properly blame your body for anything. Your body is what you make it to be. Your body is not a responsible being. It is guiltless and without blame.

Now, when a man is converted by the grace of God, regenerated, he does not get a new body; so he may look exactly the same to his neighbors, but they will recognize that a new man is living inside, and that the direction of the life has been taken over by a new driver.

A neighbor is sure to say: "Isn't that Mr. Jones who lives across the street? He was always on the way to the saloon and took up the whole sidewalk when he came back. Now he goes the other way toward the church and he has a Bible under his arm. I am sure it is the same old Jones. I recognize him."

The soul is the essential part of the man. It is the endless part of man. When the soul is converted to God, the old body begins to live a better life but it is still the same body which will dissolve and go back to dust as soon as the soul withdraws.

Let's use the illustration of what happens to a house when the residents move out and leave it unoccupied. Did you ever go out into the country and see an old, shabby house in which no one has lived for a long time?

Such an untended dwelling always goes to rot and ruin. We maintain our houses from day to day because we live in them. That is a poor illustration of a glorious fact—that as long as the soul is the tenant the body remains alive. It is when the soul withdraws that the doctors must come and pronounce that the body is dead.

With the understanding that God has given us, we have to agree that the physical body is the least essential part of the man. Some scientist has called the body "a concatenation of atoms," just a group of atoms and molecules that have gotten together for a while.

A man is more than likely to put a hat on the top of his body and walk down the street with a little strut, and say, "What a big boy am I!" But the truth is that he is just a walking concatenation of atoms and that is all.

The truth is that the soul of man is the essential part. Just as soon as the soul decides to wing away there will not be anything there for you to put your hat on. The body will decay and depart.

It is in the soul that our memory lodges and memory can either be a treasure or a terror to a man. To be suddenly called upon to remember the deeds done in the body would be a pleasure to some men but a terror to others.

Likewise with intelligence and moral perception, moral responsibility and everlastingness, hope of heaven and endless peace—all of these repose in the human soul.

My friend, you do have a soul and it is the essential part of you. It is that which speaks when you say "I."

It is that which prays when you say, "Oh God, come to me!"

It is that of which Jesus spoke when He said, "Father, into your hands I commit my spirit" (Luke 23:46). It is the essential part of man.

Soul and Spirit

Theologically there may be a distinction between soul and spirit but for all proper human purposes, I believe they are the same. In the Bible, it is plain that the word soul and the word spirit have sometimes been used synonymously as being the interior part of man, that part of man which is endless.

You do have a soul and the New Testament teaches that man's soul must be saved. It teaches that as a man saves his soul, all of his being is saved. It teaches, too, that if a man loses his own soul, everything else goes down to ruin. That is why Jesus, our Lord, gave us the caution: "What good will it be for a man if he gains the whole world, yet forfeits his soul?" (Matthew 16:26).

Jesus taught that a man must be interested in the saving of his own soul and that he has a real part in the saving of his soul.

The Apostle Peter wrote: "Save yourselves from this corrupt generation" (Acts 2:40). Save is the verb. Yourselves is the object. You is the implied subject, right?

"You save yourself," Peter was saying.

Now, do not make me a liberal over this. Peter was not so foolish as to think that a man has any antidote for his grief or that he has any kind of penances for his ills. Peter was not so foolish as to think that a man can forgive his own soul or wash his own spirit or cleanse his own inward being—he knew better.

What Peter is pointing out is this: "I preach unto you Jesus the Redeemer. You must now take advantage of the opportunity. Go to Jesus as you are and save yourself."

That is what he meant and that is what I mean. The Bible teaches that man has a responsibility in the saving of himself; that he must take advantage of the fountain that was opened in the house of David. It is the fountain for sin and uncleanness that flowed from Emmanuel's veins.

Prone to Neglect

We should realize that a man can cause his own

soul to perish through negligence. Man is prone to neglect and to procrastination and they are among the enemies of the soul. It would be wonderful indeed if everything in our world could be geared to the salvation of men's souls, but everything is geared in just the opposite direction.

Fallen nature is no friend of God. Fallen nature is no friend of God's grace. The winds that blow through the corridors of this world do not blow heavenward; they blow hellward. The man with no place of stability or anchorage goes to the way the wind blows.

Nevertheless, you have a soul to save and a God to glorify.

I find some of the theologians are no longer happy to sing Wesley's confession:

> A charge to keep I have,
> A God to glorify;
> A never-dying soul to save,
> And fit it for the sky.

These words bother their consciences and confuse their theology so they run the blue pencil through Wesley's concept of the saving of the soul and our human responsibility, as in his words: "Assured, if I my trust betray, I shall forever die."

In the old marine traditions of the world, the owner of a noble ship loaded with fabulous cargo entrusted the vessel and cargo and crew to the captain with the charge: "Bring her in. Bring her in and get your proper receipts. I want to know that you have taken her through."

In a similar sense, God has given us a serious charge: "I have given you a soul. I have given you that which is the essential part of you. You are in command of a fabulous treasure house stored with memories, imagination, rich treasure—all of these and more belong to you. I charge you that you see to it that you make that shore at last."

An old camp meeting song has these words of assurance: "I'll be present when the roll is called; I'll answer to my name."

It is through the grace and the merit of our Lord Jesus Christ that we will be appearing and answering to our name in that great day, but it will not be an appearance in this old body. The Bible does not teach us that we are going to take this particular body to heaven. The new body that God gives us is going to be somewhat like this one—only it will be a glorified body, perfect in every way.

We will all be good-looking up there because when we see Him as He is, we shall be like Him (1 John 3:2). We shall be like Him who is the Lily of the Valley and the Rose of Sharon.

When our Lord came to live among men on this earth, His deity was disguised. He wore the common garment of the peasant of Palestine. The prophet said there was "nothing in his appearance that we should desire him" (Isaiah 53:2). Then when the cruel men plucked out His beard and slapped His holy face and bruised His cheeks, He was marred more than any man in visage. They watched Him die and He was not beautiful then.

It is a different scene now. Resurrected, ascended, glorified again with the Father, He is Lord of Lords and King of Kings. All the shining stars in their splendor shine like the glory and radiance of His face. The beauty of Jesus will be upon all of His people—the redeemed, the cleansed, the forgiven who have walked in faithfulness in the light—and His name will be on their foreheads. There will be no need of the sun, for the Lamb is the light thereof (see Revelation 21:23).

We look at one another now and some of us are not too happy about these bodies in which we live. But faith and trust and hope and anticipation belong to the believer—we look confidently over into that heavenly scene with the redeemed of all ages. The brilliance and the radiance and the glory in the scene around the heavenly throne beckon to us even now—and all of this light and radiance is equivalent to and commensurate with the glory in the souls of the redeemed!

Many years ago I was in a youth service in a large church in the city of Akron and something happened that has been vivid in my memory since that day.

This was a church where there were many signs of worldliness as well as great professionalism in the choir and among the musicians. The pastor would come into the pulpit and give his well-known essays, such as "The Harp of a Thousand Strings." It did not seem that there was enough religion around there to save a mosquito even granted that he was salvageable.

But in this service I attended, they had asked a young girl to sing, and she was a hunchback, terribly deformed and twisted.

There she stood, about as high as the desk, and with her face set almost down on her breast.

Sweetly she began to sing and you knew she was singing her testimony of faith and love.

> My soul is so happy in Jesus—for He is
> so precious to me,
> Tis Heaven below, my Redeemer to
> know,
> For He is so precious to me.

Then when she came into the last verse she sounded the personal word of her experience and hope in the faith:

> Where, some day, through faith in His
> wonderful grace,
> I know I'll be like Him, and look on His
> face.

A little hunchback girl—not much to look at, sickly and pale, deformed in physical body, but radiant in soul and spirit because she had grasped the promise that one day she will be like Him, laying her cross and her burden down!

I dare you to show me anything better than that! Take a fine-tooth comb and search through the cultures and the treasures of the world and you will still not come up with any kind of a jewel that will shine like that simple testimony of faith and hope in the beauty of the soul!

It makes no difference who we are or where we live or the status we may have in life—if we have placed our faith and trust in our glorified Savior we will receive an eternal tabernacle worthy of our soul for it will be a body like unto His glorified body.

What have you ever heard in this life that can compare with that promise?

Don't let the devil rob you of the glory that God has promised and prepared. All around you fallen human nature is determined that your soul will not be saved and fallen society is determined that it is not going to let you live a happy, faithful Christian life.

In these days we must stand fast in witnessing and living forth the evangelical gospel. We believe in the purifying power of the blood of Jesus. We believe in the grace and mercy of God. We believe in the power of Christ's gospel to make a bad man good and a dirty man clean; to make the evil man righteous and the sinful man pure.

Yes, man has a soul to save and amid all the creature noises around us, there is the still, small voice within man, saying, "Be reconciled to God" (2 Corinthians 5:20). That is the real "you" under the camouflage—it is that "you" that will take you to heaven or hell!

What can we do but look to Him as Savior, and say, "Jesus, lover of my soul, let me to Thy bosom fly."

The Fate of the Moral Fool:
He Goes Where He Belongs

*He said to him, "If they do not listen to Moses
and the Prophets, they will not be convinced, even
if someone rises from the dead." (Luke 16:31)*

Man is a moral wanderer in this present
world—but he becomes a moral fool when
he has shut out the voice of God and flippantly
consoles himself with the excuse: "Well, if I go to
hell, I will have plenty of company!"

The moral fool who goes to hell will be
surprised indeed to find that hell has its own
ways of singling out a man, isolating him from
everything that would be a comfort. I am convinced that the lost man who spurns the call of
God in this life will suffer all alone in his lostness
in hell—completely alone and unsupported and
uncomforted!

Now, in this world, people try to take their comfort in strange ways.

It seems to be comforting to many that even if they are bad and they know it, they can always insist that everyone else is bad, too!

Some people actually find comfort in hiding behind verses from the Bible that teach that men are lost. One of the favorite proof texts is Romans 3:22: "For all have sinned and fall short of the glory of God."

That is the prime text for the Bible school student who is studying how to win souls in ten easy lessons, and we quote it often in the attempt to bring conviction to the lost soul.

But in many cases it turns out to be a comforting verse to the sinner. Because of the treachery of the human soul, it is possible to hide behind the fact that all have sinned. There is a kind of universal reaction which becomes an acceptable philosophy; that "if this is what is wrong with everybody, then nobody need worry about it."

Therefore, when I say that man is a moral wanderer, away from God and still hiding, I do not want you to hide behind that and take comfort in it. I want you to know that it is a very personal thing and that the Holy Spirit never meant to give anyone a sense of comfort in universal depravity.

Actually, the Holy Spirit is saying throughout the Scriptures: "Thou art the man!"

God is calling us with many, many voices, but there is no doubt that He entreats mankind most perfectly in the revealed Word of God.

A Glimpse of Hell

In the sixteenth chapter of Luke's gospel, we have recorded the words of our Lord Jesus Christ concerning the pleading of the rich man who died and was suffering in hell. There must have been many who were in hell, but you will notice that when the rich man went there he could not find any comfort. He was alone. As far as he was concerned, there was no one else there.

The only people he knew and remembered were those who were still alive.

Let me remind you again that it is Jesus the Christ, Jesus the Lord of all the world and of life and of death and of eternity, who gave us this vivid picture of the pleading from hell. He drew aside the opaque curtain to let us see and hear what had never before been communicated to living men and women.

He let us hear the actual words of a condemned man. This is the only place in the Bible where we meet an eternally condemned man and hear him speak, almost as if we are looking into his face.

Strangely and wonderfully, this lost man becomes an evangelist whose voice still remains a powerful entreaty—the sovereign God showing that hell itself as well as the spirits in heaven will ultimately bow and own God's right and own the righteousness of His ways.

There is more in this account than the suffering of the rich man—there is also the blessedness of the beggar who at his death was carried by the angels to Abraham's bosom.

There was a contrast between the two in their lifetime. The beggar was a poor fellow, with sores and diseases, and he had to beg crumbs from the rich man's table.

You will notice in the account that Jesus said nothing bad about the rich man. I do not see how you can make a rascal out of this rich man. He had plenty of material goods, but the Bible does not charge him with stealing. He might have gotten it with all honesty. He just had it, that's all.

He did live sumptuously—but you and I do, too. If we have it, we spend it—and if we do not have it, we grumble. Our society is guilty of throwing money right and left, billions upon billions.

These are the things I want you to notice: the beggar was not saved because of his poverty and certainly the rich man did not go to hell because he was a rich man!

No one in this world has ever been saved and gone to heaven because he was poor. You can be as poor as a church mouse and still be as bad as a church rat. God has never said anywhere that human poverty is a means of salvation. Poverty never redeemed any man. Wearing rags in this life never has gotten anybody into heaven. That claim is only poetic, religious nonsense!

The poor beggar did not go to heaven because he was poor and a beggar. If that had been true, then salvation would depend upon poverty and rags and you would be able to tell how near a man is to heaven by the size of his bank account or by the lack of it. That would make religion a completely human thing, which it is not.

Would a beggar lie? Would a poor man cheat? God says that every liar will have his part in hell. God talks about human hearts that are unclean and deceitful and treacherous. So, you can have rags and sores and be hungry and still be on the road to hell.

Neither did the rich man go to hell because he happened to have plenty of material things in this life. That would be to equate eternity with time and to judge that God is going to take all of the rich people who have enjoyed themselves down here and send them to hell for eternity. God has made it plain enough that that is not the way He does things.

We will never know the number of wealthy men and women whom God has honored for their faith, for their Christian testimony, for their unselfishness in their stewardship.

You study the Bible and the plan of salvation and the lives of God's great souls among men and you will reject the thesis that men and women go to hell because they are rich and that others go to heaven because they are poor.

Oh, that would be the simplest thing in the world!

"Throw everything of this world's goods away, strip down to bare necessities and flap your wings—you will soon be in the celestial city; for God is going to punish eternally all those who have money in this life!"

Oh, no! No! That is too simple and it destroys moral and spiritual values and ignores completely man's spiritual nature.

Let me tell you why this beggar went to heaven and why this certain rich man went to hell.

This beggar went to heaven because he had a nature that belonged there. This rich man went to hell because he had a nature that belonged there.

That is it—and there is no other answer!

The beggar was carried by the angels into Abraham's bosom and I ask, "What were those angels doing down there?" Those angels had all the vast universe in which to roam, but some of them turned up at the curbstone when that poor beggar rolled over and groaned, closed his eyes, and said, "Father, here I come."

Now, God cannot have a disembodied soul that He has redeemed and that carries His nature in it, roaming like a ghost through the universe. The angels do the will of God and when the body died, the angels escorted his soul, winging away with it to Abraham's bosom.

Why? Because it belonged there!

Where It Belongs

Remember this: everything must be put in its place in God's universe at last. A man can be living with another man's wife now, but there will be a day when God will put every man where he belongs. Some official may have the widow's property now, but the day will come when God will put everything where it belongs.

That is the picture that God gave Ezekiel of the valley of dry bones. The bones were all out of place—the jackals and buzzards had worked them over for years. But when the Word of the Lord came unto them there was a great rattling and God put everything in order.

God carries out His own plans and He has promised that everything will be put in order. Right now we live in a confused and mixed-up world. Some people get the headlines who, if the truth were known, should be getting a striped suit in a prison somewhere.

There are other worthy persons who are completely ignored in this world and, if the truth were known, they would be on the front covers of the news magazines next week.

God is not mixed up, though. God is not confused! God continues to watch the human scene and He has His own process for sorting things out. Many a person receiving the praise and plaudits of the world today will be sorted out when God's time comes. He does not sort them out down here in our time. He did not even sort them when His twelve disciples were with Him. Peter was a coward and Judas was a lover of money and a betrayer, but not until the last minute did He even mention it. But when Judas died he was sorted out. He died and went to his own place.

Death sorts us out and if we go to heaven it is because we have a nature that belongs there. It is not hard for the sovereign God to sort out all the natures that belong in heaven and take them there.

In essence, that is the story of Lazarus the beggar and the rich man.

What kind of nature do you have? That is where the decision is made.

The rich man had been intent upon the things of this life. He felt no need of seeking God with his inner nature and that was his sin. That is what stamped him as a lost man.

On the other hand, do not imagine for a moment that all of those old boys down on Skid Row, down and out, will all go to heaven when they die, like a flock of birds at sunset. God will know where they belong by their inner natures, by decisions they have made either to know and love God or to ignore and reject Him.

Now, a fool is someone who acts without regard to consequences; a moral fool is one who never hears any of the voices that are calling to him. He has ears to hear but he hears not.

In His time of ministry on the earth, Jesus told many of those who listened to His teachings that they were fulfilling the prophecy of Isaiah that "this people's heart has become calloused; they hardly hear with their ears, and they have closed their eyes. Otherwise they might see with their eyes, hear with their ears, understand with their hearts and turn, and I would heal them" (Matthew 13:15).

Then with a tender look to His few beloved disciples around Him, He said: But blessed are your eyes because they see, and your ears because they hear" (13:16).

The moral fool never hears anything from God. To him, there is no tongue in any tree, no book in any running brook, no sermon in any stone, and no voice in anything.

He is satisfied just to go his own way in this world. He compares one nice automobile with another. He is figuring out how much he can make on his next deal. He is figuring close and cutting corners on his income tax. He has to spend a little time every day with the baseball standings or the football statistics.

He is just spending his time—he is not a bad man. He is just a moral fool—he never hears the important voices in life.

Oh, if he gets sick, he hears something within that says, "Get to a doctor as quick as you can." Or, if he gets into financial trouble, he hears the voices of friends who say, "I know a good broker," or, "I know a good banker."

But he hears no voice from God. He is living for this world and for this world alone. If he can keep reasonably healthy, keep his hair on his head, drive a car with "good rubber," he is satisfied.

He is a moral fool!

A Great Contrast

What a great contrast in this world between the moral fool and those who are morally wise.

Someone who was supposed to be smart once said that the Christian gospel is all right—but that no one has ever really tried it.

We thank God that that statement is not really

true—we are not going to apologize and fall for that. No one should think for even a split second that the gospel of Jesus Christ is not having its effect or that God does not have His redeemed people all over the world.

We will never admit that the ark was not effective because only eight people got into it and were saved.

We do not apologize for the ark—it worked. Those who tried it found that it worked and they made fools of the millions who rejected and ignored what God said about it.

So, those who are morally wise do hear the entreating voice of God. They always have and they always will—they are hearing that voice now.

God Almighty does not bellow to the wide universe and have it come back as an empty echo through His holy ears. He has told us that His word going forth from His mouth does not ever return void and without results. God's word is always powerful and it needs no one to run around apologizing for it and thinking up clever ways to defend it.

The gospel ship, the ark of God, is not a ghost ship floating idly on the sea. Thank God, she has a full crew and she has her passengers. There are not as many as God wants and there is still room for more. Snap to attention when you see the sails of this mighty ship on the horizon. Fully manned with a faithful crew, the winds of the Holy Spirit in her sails, passengers who are no longer slaves but free men and women, bound for a free port in a holy land!

Throughout this troubled old world, God has His saints and He knows them. They are washed in His blood, born of His Spirit. They are begotten of the Word of Truth, saved by the miracle of redemption. He will call them all home when the time comes.

That brings us back to Luke 16 and the rich man in hell.

I think we would have to say that he was a better man after he was dead than he was while he lived.

While he lived, he did not care or show concern for anyone around him. He did not have much sympathy for other people. But in the region of the lost he began to be concerned for his brother, "so that they will not also come to this place of torment" (Luke 16:28).

He was an evangelist making an altar call from hell—only he did not get through.

Note also that he had had religious connections when he was alive. He called Abraham "Father" and Abraham did not disallow it. Abraham was able to say, "Son, remember." He was a son of Abraham's flesh from a Jewish environment, the most religious nation in the world.

But Abraham had to tell him that those still living "have Moses and the Prophets; let them listen to them" (16:29).

God knows the human conscience. He knows that the most effective voice throughout the world is the voice of the Word. If men will not hear the Word of God, they will not hear anything else.

A religious environment, a religious connection—these are not enough. If we could hear them, if they could get through to us now, I have no doubt that there would be voices and the warnings of many who are departed from us. It is not enough to belong to the church board, to be an elder, a deacon, an usher.

How many, how many, if they could tell us now, would say: "I was a moral fool while I lived. I refused to take God's call seriously. Send someone to my brothers and sisters, to my children, to warn them!"

The wise voice of God and Abraham said, "No, it is no use. A church officer who can receive communion and handle funds and lead in prayer and hear the Word of God preached and still resists Me—even if I sent a dead man back he would not listen!"

Yes, the morally wise will hear this, for "the wonder of life is the moral law within and the starry heavens above."

The moral life within—that is, our moral constitution—provides always an eloquent, accusing, pleading, and entreating voice. The message is always from the heart of God, "Oh, return unto Me!"

CHAPTER 9

Our Accountability to God: Justified, Saved—But on Trial

For it is time for judgment to begin with the family of God; and if it begins with us, what will the outcome be for those who do not obey the gospel of God? (1 Peter 4:17)

Throughout the Christian church as we know it today, all sense of accountability to God seems to have been lost.

This must be blamed on preaching and teaching which has overemphasized the "automatic" quality of faith, with the insistence that "acceptance of Christ" passes all responsibility and all accountability from the believer to the Savior—for all time to come!

Christians no longer sing with very much feeling that hymn of Charles Wesley's that asks our Lord to:

> Arm me with jealous care
>   As in Thy sight to live;
> And Oh, Thy servant, Lord, prepare
>   A strict account to give.

Someone has been quoted recently as saying: "If I believed that I had to give an accounting of my service as seen in the eyes of God, I could never be happy!"

A lot of people will not know what we are talking about, but let me tell you about Charles Wesley, who breathed that sincere and holy prayer that he would be able to give a strict account to God.

He was a Christian believer who was only one jump short of being hysterically happy in the Lord. Dr. Samuel Johnson, the great English philologist and critic, said of John and Charles Wesley in their day: "They are the loftiest examples of complete moral happiness that I have ever seen."

I read the hymns of Charles Wesley and I admit that I find myself chuckling with delight. I believe he was so spiritually happy that he must have danced for joy—happy in God and in Christ!

Yet, he believed he was still on spiritual probation. He could write and sing,

> Arise, my soul, arise!
>   Shake off thy guilty fears;
> The bleeding Sacrifice
>   In my behalf appears.

> Before the throne my Surety stands:
> My name is written on His hands.

The modern church can join in that expression of faith but finds it very difficult to sing with Wesley,

> Arm me with jealous care
> As in Thy sight to live;
> And Oh, Thy servant, Lord, prepare
> A strict account to give.

Now, I do not know how men and women can excuse themselves completely as though one of the voices of God sounding throughout the earth is not the voice of judgment. I have searched the Word again for this message, and I have not been able to get away from the fact of judgment as it pertains to the house of God, to Christians rather than to sinners.

It is well for us to consider here that church history shows plainly that religious people are prone to select a favorite Bible doctrine or truth and to hold to that one truth at the expense of other basic tenets. We may overemphasize that one truth so as to obscure other important truths which may actually disappear as a result.

This is what I mean by a truth disappearing—it falls into disuse and therefore is easily forgotten.

I would illustrate that.

Suppose there is one key on the piano that is not properly attached and it gives forth no sound when it is struck. The pianist is sure to be wincing when he strikes that key and nothing happens. If you would photograph the keyboard, that key would be in its proper place in the picture, but it will not produce any sound no matter how hard you touch it.

That is an illustration of what I mean by a basic doctrine of the Christian faith that has fallen into disuse, so that it is no longer talked about or thought about or preached about. If you go to the book of discipline, the statement of doctrine, you will find it still in place because it will say that we do firmly hold this truth.

But it no longer plays—it is no longer heard. It has no emphasis and no power because it is slurred over and forgotten. That is how a basic Bible truth may fall into disuse because certain doctrines have been overemphasized to the obscuring of others.

Reassert a Forgotten Truth

Then, finally, some prophet of God has to come and reassert the forgotten truths and reemphasize and trumpet them forth. That person may be considered a heretic because that segment of Bible truth has been obscured for a generation or two.

But in the midst of the grumbling, the prophet of God keeps persisting until the church awakes and readopts that truth so that a new sense of life comes as if it were raised from the dead.

Think of Martin Luther. Did he invent a new doctrine? No, he did not. Luther dug out a doctrine that had fallen into a dismal tomb and was not being heard. By sounding the trumpet blast of justification by faith, Luther brought about the great Reformation.

What did John Wesley do? He did not invent any new doctrine by sounding forth a forgotten doctrine that it is possible to have and to know purity of heart; he aroused the church!

Men who have been used of God in any generation from Calvary down to this hour have not invented and preached new truths. They have simply had the anointed vision to discover truths that had been obscured by the overemphasis of certain other truths.

Now, that is introductory to say this: that justification by faith has become such a doctrine in our time. It has been emphasized to a point where it has obscured certain other closely related truths; so we have lost the cutting power of those truths.

I know it would be difficult for any man to be eloquent enough to overstate the vital importance of justification by faith in the Christian church— that man will live by his faith and not by works of righteousness which he has done. Therefore, being justified by faith we have peace with God!

Justification by faith delivers us from the fruitless struggle to be good. It delivers us from the bondage of the Pharisees and the pride of the ritualist and the snare of the legalist—all of whom attempt in many human ways to make themselves presentable to God.

But those are just old Adam decking himself out in his best religious garments for the sake of impressing God Almighty, hoping to be ushered in at last as a man who served God faithfully all the days of his life.

That is the bondage some of our fathers fell into because the doctrine of justification by faith was obscured. It was dropped out of the teaching of the church. So, the people had to have holy water and holy beads and holy everything. They had sacred hearts of this and sacred hearts of that. They had days to eat and days to abstain from eating and they tried to make themselves acceptable to God by gifts of money and doing penance for their sins.

Then along came a thoughtful scholar in the Scriptures. He presented no new truth or doctrine, but insisted on the reexamination of an old Bible truth, long buried and forgotten, proclaiming that it is not by our works of righteousness, but it is by faith through grace that we can be pleasing to God.

Immediately, the reformation was born!

The Church of Christ got up out of a long sleep and like the dry bones in Ezekiel's vision, she stood up and walked as a great army. Then, with the passing of the years, that doctrine of justification by faith has been emphasized until it has been thrown out of focus as badly as was the opposite before Luther's time.

As a result, justification as it is now understood and preached and emphasized and hammered on up and down the country, is causing believers to throw all responsibility over on God, and we conceive ourselves to be happy, satisfied Christians without a responsibility in the world except to give out a tract once in a while.

It becomes just an automatic thing—you simply get in the Pullman sleeper, pull down the bed out of the wall, and wake up in the depot in heaven. All judgment has been bypassed, for Christians are not thinking of judgment any more.

I discover that the average Christian now seems to have only one worry—he is concerned that he might lose what we call "fellowship."

In that case, he might not be as happy tomorrow as he was today or as happy day after tomorrow as he was yesterday. He wants to be a happy little moron, with the result that he says, "I must learn to keep up my fellowship so I will be happy."

Accountable to God

The idea that a believer is accountable to God for the deeds done in the body has completely passed out of the theological thinking of the modern fundamentalist church. Faith has become a kind of magic having beneficial properties which accrue to the man who believes—and they accrue to him no matter what his state in life may be. He believes—therefore they accrue. There is no longer any consideration of the moral condition of the man, whether or not he is obedient, whether or not he is faithful to God or what kind of Christian he is.

He believes or he has believed—therefore the automatic benefits of this magic faith accrue to him now and in the world to come.

Now, this kind of teaching has obscured other truth, so it is a true doctrine pushed out of focus. It is a doctrine of grace and justification by faith alone pushed by uncorrected logic to a ridiculous and grotesque conclusion.

The Bible truth that has been obscured and buried and forgotten as a result, is the doctrine of probation. We seldom hear anything about it any more and a man who wants to consider it and talk about it and turn back to the Bible teaching is made to feel very much like a heretic.

Let us consider what we mean by our Christian lives here being a probation period.

We mean that this life is a preparation for the next and that preparation is not concluded when we come to the Lord Jesus Christ for our salvation.

We read in the Gospels that the thief on the cross believed and the dying Savior told him that he would be in paradise the same day. We make that to be the criterion by which we judge the entire transaction of believing faith. We believe in Christ and thus we are prepared for heaven, and there is no such thing as probation or a testing or any judgment to come—nothing like that now in modern theology!

That is why I have said that it is possible to emphasize a good doctrine to the point that it may overshadow and cause another truth to disappear. In this case, it has gone so far that leading teachers now take the position that the doctrine of probation and spiritual preparation is not biblical. They insist that everything is cared for by one act of faith and there is no such thing as an expectation of judgment to come.

Certainly we are all agreed that faith in Jesus Christ has settled many important things forever. Our faith in Christ has settled forever our past sin—it is forgiven. Our faith in Christ has settled forever our justification before the Father in heaven. It has settled forever that our names are written in the Lamb's book of life. It has settled forever that we are regenerated men and women and the seed of God is in us.

These are things that are settled and made sure by an abiding faith in Christ.

But the great mistake in our day is the total disregard for the fact that believing Christians are on probation from day to day, proving the character of our faith and testing and preparing us for the world to come.

Certainly our Father in heaven has a great interest in what we will do with this gracious spiritual life and new nature we have been given. Certainly He will be testing our obedience to the Word; our faithfulness to Him who has died for us; what we will be doing with our time and gifts, our opportunities and our possessions.

The Apostle Paul plainly taught the believers in Rome that "each of us will give an account of himself to God" (Romans 14:12).

He wrote to the Corinthian believers that "[every man's] work will be shown for what it is, because the Day will bring it to light. It will be revealed with fire, and the fire will test the quality of each man's work" (1 Corinthians 3:13).

The quality of our Christian life is sure to be affected if we do not feel that we are going to give an account to God of how we have used time and abilities and money and possessions He has entrusted to us.

The response of some Christians is: "Just stay out of my business—I will do what I please with my time and with my money."

I know that—and yet I also know that God is testing them and He is going to find out if they have enough moral sense to know what to do with time. Time is a treasured gift which God has given us but He has not given it to use foolishly.

The results of this time of testing will be seen in that great and coming day before the judgment seat of Christ. Someone has written that the Apostle Paul surely lived with one eye on the judgment seat of Christ and the other on the perishing world.

Saved, But on Probation

Every Christian is saved—but many have forgotten that they are still on trial. They have forgotten that the Bible has much to say about that "great day" when every man's work will be revealed. They are so happy that they are saved that they have forgotten that God is testing moral wisdom and moral courage, testing faithfulness and vision and stewardship for the kind of times in which we live.

We could spend hours describing the dark side

of the times in which we live—but I would remind you that they are God's gift to us. We know that crime and corruption are found throughout the nation. We know that many conditions make our country a top-heavy country, and that we could come crashing down as other nations and empires have in the past.

But I do not wish myself in any other period of the world's history. These times are God Almighty's gift to me as a Christian, and I consider myself on probation, sensing that God is really interested in what one of the least of His servants is going to do about the times in which he lives.

Justified and saved—but on trial: that is where the Christian should hold himself. But we are so eager to get out from under all responsibility we kick up our irresponsible heels like an unbroken colt and snort our defiance of all judgment.

We are not living in a period of God's expressed judgment at this time, and that is why man thinks he can get away with almost everything now. If this were a period of divine judgment, you would sin and the Lord would punish you immediately. He would prove to you immediately that you were not worthy of His kingdom.

But this is a period of probation and the Holy Spirit says, "Therefore judge nothing before the appointed time; wait till the Lord comes. He will bring to light what is hidden in darkness and will expose the motives of men's hearts. At that time each will receive his praise from God" (4:5).

This period in which we live is not the trial—it is

the preparation for the trial. This is not the last examination—this is getting ready for the examination.

I remind you that this whole doctrine has been long obscured, but our Lord Jesus set it forth fully in Matthew 25.

Jesus tells the story there of the man who went into a far country and before leaving, called in his three servants. He gave them talents to be held in trust during his absence. He gave one man five talents, another two and another one, each according to his ability. They could not complain for each was given what he deserved.

Then he said, "I will be coming back—remember that I have delivered unto you my goods."

The servants who had received five and two talents began to use that which had been entrusted to them. The third servant buried his talent in the ground.

Then, when the master returned, he called his servants in for an accounting. He wanted their reports.

Consider that while he was gone they could have done just as they pleased. They could have done what they pleased with the responsibility. But two of them realized that they were actually on probation while the third did not.

Two of them said, "We have used your money wisely; here it is with interest."

The third said, "I was afraid so I hid the money in the ground."

The master said to the first two, "You have been

faithful over a few things, I will make you ruler over many."

The third servant, who did not realize that he would actually be on trial during the master's absence, was cast out as an unprofitable servant.

What are you going to do with that passage?

As God's sheep, many of us have discovered that the green pastures of His provision are spiritually satisfying wherever we find them in His book. I like one of the standing rules at the Moody Bible Institute: "The Word of God may not be all about me, but it is all for me!"

I consider this an eloquent argument to me about the rest of my Christian life down here. How can we argue that our day-by-day service to God and to our fellow men is not being sharply scrutinized and that it will not be severely judged before the feet of Jesus Christ in that great day?

The believer is justified and saved from that awful appearance before the great white throne judgment, where the lost of all the ages will be judged.

But the hour will come when our kindly-faced but serious Savior will call the redeemed and justified to His feet, saying: "I must have an account of the deeds done in the body since you were saved. You have had more abilities entrusted to you than many. You have had many opportunities to shine as a star in the darkness of the times. You have had months and years entrusted to you for faithful and obedient service and witness."

There will be no place to hide then. You tried to settle everything in the spiritual life by one act of believing but there are some things that are never settled until death cuts us off or until the Lord comes.

Now what is it that God expects of us, morally, and spiritually?

He advises the way of self-judgment: "If we judged ourselves we would not come under judgment" (11:31).

He expects us to be obedient children of God, knowing that it takes a moral determination to obey Him in day-by-day faithfulness.

But that is where our spiritual happiness lies.

I trust many more of us are becoming willing to breathe sincerely that prayer with Charles Wesley:

> Arm me with jealous care
> As in Thy sight to live;
> And Oh, Thy servant, Lord, prepare
> A strict account to give.

CHAPTER 10

Jesus Is More Than Savior: Finally, He Will Be the Judge

For as the Father has life in himself, so he has granted the Son to have life in himself. And he has given him authority to judge because he is the Son of Man. (John 5:26-27)

Someone could write a very important book for our day on great Bible doctrines that are either forgotten or neglected.

One of these themes neglected and overlooked is the fact that Jesus Christ Himself is the judge of all mankind.

Jesus plainly told the generation of His own day that the Father in heaven will not judge anyone but "has entrusted all judgment to the Son" (John 5:22).

It is a tragedy that so many men and women live among us and die in their time without ever coming to the knowledge that our Lord Jesus Christ is both the Savior and the judge of all mankind.

When we discover all of the implications of this vital truth we discover as well that we both love Him and fear Him. We love Him because He is our Savior, and we fear and reverence Him because He knows all about us and knows all that is in us, and to Him has been committed all judgment.

I find myself indignant concerning much preaching and teaching which portrays the Christ as a soft and pliant friend of everybody, a painted, plastic figure without any spine and involved in no way with justice. If that is the only Christ there is, we might as well close our books and shut our doors and let them make a garage or shop of the church building.

But that Christ that is being so preached is not the Christ of God, not the Christ of the Bible, nor the Christ who will actually deal with mankind. That Christ has eyes as a flaming fire; His feet are like burnished brass and from His mouth comes a sharp, two-edged sword. He will be the judge of mankind.

The blessed part of that is that Christian believers may leave their loved ones who have died in His hands, knowing that He Himself has suffered; knowing that He knows all and that no mistakes can be made in that day of revelation and judgment.

Now, this has been introductory to our consideration of basic concepts of judgment as found in the Word of God, to some of the human and inadequate points of judgment, and to the qualifications of Jesus Christ for the final judgment of mankind.

Morally Accountable

There is a basic concept of judgment, a simple concept held by practically all of the religious people that have ever lived anywhere, with variations in the details. This is the belief that human beings are morally accountable because they are not self-created beings, nor self-sustaining. Their life is derived from another and not from themselves.

God, the Father in heaven, does have life in Himself; so, no one can judge the Father. He is not a derived being—He is the original being.

Jesus infuriated His critics in His time when He taught that the heavenly Father had also given to the Son this quality of having life in Himself. Jesus Christ is not a derived being but is of the Father alone. No one can judge the Son.

It is not inconsistent for us to believe that men are free to decide their own moral choices while believing at the same time that they are also under the necessity to account to God for those choices. That makes them both free and also bound; for they are bound to come to judgment and give an account for the deeds done in the body.

Let us look at some of the inadequate concepts of judgment which are often taught among us.

Probably the first is this: the operation of the law of compensation.

Ralph Waldo Emerson in his essays espoused the teaching that there is no such thing as a judgment to come; that everything is judged and sentenced and rewarded or punished in the present.

The basis of this position is that if you take something from your left pocket, you compensate by putting it in your right pocket, and that everything that you do in one direction is counterbalanced by something done in the opposite direction.

Using this premise, Emerson said that the thief steals from himself, and his punishment is the knowledge that he is a thief.

There is a portion of truth in that, but it is not enough. It is an inadequate concept of judgment and it is not taught anywhere in the Bible.

Another inadequate concept is that we are judged only by public opinion.

Of course, we are all responsible to public opinion in some ways but it is rather silly for men and women to argue that there is no other judgment than that which public opinion may impose.

You live beside your neighbor and certainly he is going to judge you as to whether or not you have been a good neighbor. You drive your car on the highway and others will conclude either that you are a good driver or that you are a miserable road hog.

But to argue that final judgment rests with public opinion is to argue like a backward child—for something more is yet to come.

Others have taken the position that judgment rests completely with human law. Every nation teaches that citizens are accountable to human law. Every nation makes its laws—and that is true from the most primitive tribes of New Guinea to the most civilized nations of the world. They have their own laws and all are made responsible to those laws.

"But," you say, "what about the outlaw?"

Generally, he is an outlaw in only a few things. An outlaw may rob a bank in order to get money to pay his legal taxes. He is breaking one law while he is keeping another. Nevertheless, he is an outlaw and is accountable to the law even while he is breaking it. The law has no way of equitably punishing all of those who have broken the bounds of various human restrictions.

You have also probably heard someone say that "man is accountable to society." There is a measure of truth here, as well, but the problem is that society cannot reach us in that sphere of our being where we are most vitally accountable— namely, to God and to ourselves.

I live in an American city. I am accountable to public opinion. I am accountable to the laws of the land. But I am also accountable to myself and to my God.

Thus, in the relationships which are the most vital to me, human society cannot touch me at all.

The man who says, "I will commit suicide," and then turns the gun to his head and kills himself, is no longer accountable to society and will not answer to the law—but he is still accountable to some higher authority.

A man stands up and proclaims that he is an atheist and turns his back on God. There is not a country anywhere in the world that will punish a man for that—not a country in the world that will punish a man for hating God.

Some countries have punished men for not going to church and for not paying the assessed ecclesiastical tax, but men can hate God in their hearts and never be punished because human society cannot reach them in that vital and important realm.

Now, there have always been those who insist that man's accountability is to himself alone—that every man stands before the bar of his own reason and of his conscience. This belief insists that man's own reason and man's conscience are both jury and judge—that each man is a law unto himself.

This gets directly into the infamous relativity of morals now being taught so widely in our educational processes. It says that a thing is good if it brings social approval and that it is evil if it brings social disapproval.

If this concept were true, then we would have as many moral codes as there are human beings. Each of us would be our own witness, our own prosecutor, our own judge, our own jury and our jailer.

In this framework of our own humanity, that concept is so silly and so inadequate that we do not find it worthy of any consideration.

To some humans it may sound very learned and very mystical but it is ridiculous—what man could ever be that honest and that hard on himself?

I know that if I were to be my own prosecutor and judge and executioner I would find some way to lose my axe. I know I would not cut my own head off.

Well, that is not the way it is going to be!

Accountable to God

Every one of us is going to be finally accountable to the One who gave us being. We are accountable to the One from whose heart we came and who laid His laws upon us. We are accountable to God!

This is the concept of accountability and morality and transformation that makes men right, that makes character, and that makes nations that can endure.

On the other hand, it is the absence of this belief that makes Christian profession soft and spineless and produces churches without any meaning in them.

A young man in our Sunday school told of visiting a church in another state where the discussions are about books, about dreams—and on the Sunday he visited, about peptic ulcers! I would get an ulcer if I stayed around a church like that.

When we backslide from the truth and run away from the Word of God we will build up our own notions out of our own heads—and there is no telling what fools we will become.

I believe it can be quickly and simply seen that when we refuse and get farther and farther away from the concept of God's judgment that the judgment of God actually begins to fall.

It was the belief in the accountability of man to his maker that made America a great nation. Among those earlier leaders was Daniel Webster whose blazing eyes and fiery oratory often held the Senate spellbound. In those days the Congress was composed of strong, noble statesmen who carried the weight of the nation in their hearts and minds.

Someone asked, "Mr. Webster, what do you consider the most serious thought that has ever entered your mind?"

"The most solemn thought that has ever entered my mind is my accountability to my Maker," he replied.

Men like that cannot be corrupted and bought. They do not have to worry if someone listens to their telephone calls. What they are in character and in deportment results from their belief that they will finally be accountable to God.

I know I do not need to remind you that the judge of all mankind must have certain qualifications, notably, the authority to execute judgment. The simple meaning of this is that those who are to be judged must be accountable to the Judge.

According to the Scriptures, to be a judge in the kingdom of God requires a kind of righteousness which goes beyond the legal structures of man. The judge of all mankind does not pronounce a verdict based upon laws enacted and imposed by someone else, as in this tentative and provisionary world in which we live. Here, one group of men will make the law and the judge, born a hundred or two hundred years later, may enforce the law and not be even remotely acquainted with the person who is being judged.

In order to be a righteous judge of mankind, the judge must himself have all knowledge so that there can be no error and no mistake.

In our earthly systems, many an innocent man has been hanged and many a person has died behind prison walls paying a debt he had never contracted, while the rascal who committed the crime died in his bed surrounded by his friends.

Human justice tries to do its best, but because there is no judge who is all-wise, such mistakes are made.

But God Almighty is never going to judge the race of mankind and allow a single soul to plead that an error has been made.

The judge must be the one who has all wisdom—therefore I appeal away from Paul. I appeal away from Moses and Elijah. I appeal away from all men because no man knows me well enough to judge me finally.

We humans may pass brief judgments on one another in simple matters here but when it comes to facing my eternal and everlasting future I do not want any possibility of human mistake.

The judge of mankind must necessarily be someone who will never need the testimony of a third party; he will not depend upon the testimony of another to make his judgment.

Listen to what Jesus said: "By myself I can do nothing; I judge only as I hear, and my judgment is just, for I seek not to please myself but him who sent me" (John 5:30).

There is another point involved here: the judge has to be disinterested. He must have no personal interest or bias. The motive and actions of some judges in this life may be brought into question, but the Son of God is able to say: "I judge as one who seeks not his own glory but the glory of God alone" (author's loose paraphrase of John 8:50).

Therefore, He can be the judge. He is personally related and yet He is disinterested—He has nothing to gain or lose by His judgment and all the glory belongs to God. Jesus Christ, therefore, qualifies to become the judge of all mankind.

Beyond that, there is the matter of the judge having a sympathetic understanding.

I do not want to be judged by an archangel that never shed a tear: I do not want to be judged by a seraph that never felt pain. I do not want to be judged by a cherub that never knew human grief or disappointment or woe.

It is plain in the record that the Father in heaven has given the Son power and authority to execute judgment because He is the Son of man. Because He is the Son of man, He can be the advocate, the Savior, by the throne of love, but He can also be the judge to sit upon the throne.

In that great day still to come, there will be no dodging, no whimpering, no whining. No one will be able to charge Him, saying, "But Lord, you did not understand!"

He does understand because He became one of us and walked among us. There was never a tear that He did not shed; never a bit of disappointment that He did not feel; never a temptation that did not come to Him; never a critical situation over which He was not victor. Christ qualifies on every count to be the judge of mankind. The tears He shed and the pains He suffered and the griefs He bore made Him not only a just but a sympathetic judge of mankind.

More than once Jesus said, "For judgment I have come into this world" (John 9:39), and He added: "For judgment I have come into this world, so that the blind will see and those who see will become blind." His presence in the human race is our present judgment of sin. When our Lord, the Son of man, comes in clouds of glory, then the nations will be gathered unto Him. He will separate them, for it is He who is to be the judge. He will have the shoulders of a man and the face of a man and He will be a man—the man, Christ Jesus.

People shrug Him off now and drive away in a cloud of fumes—but one day they will have to come back and deal with Him finally. We may be sure of one thing—He will either be our Savior now or our judge then.

Think with me about the implications of sin and judgment and repentance and forgiveness in these well-known words of Isaac Watts:

> Not all the blood of beasts
>   On Jewish altars slain,
> Could give the guilty conscience peace
>   Or wash away the stain.

Where is the authority for that? Read the eighth and tenth chapters of the book of Hebrews.

> But Christ, the heavenly Lamb,
> Takes all our sins away;
> A sacrifice of nobler name
> And richer blood than they.

It is fundamental in our Christian belief and theology that the precious blood of Jesus Christ takes away all sin.

> My faith would lay her hand
> On that dear head of Thine,
> While like a penitent I stand,
> And there confess my sin.

Surely we recognize this picture? In the Old Testament scene, the sinner would come to the priest and he would say, "I have sinned and I bring a lamb," or some other animal. The priest would accept that creature and the sinner would lay his hand on the head of the beast as the priest killed it and sprinkled the blood. Thus, in that day, the sin which had been committed was forgiven.

> My soul looks back to see
> The burden Thou did'st bear,
> When hanging on th' accursed tree,
> And knows her guilt was there.

Do we really believe that? That it was our guilt there on that accursed tree? Yes, it was true that "God made him who knew no sin to be sin for us, so that in him we might become the righteousness of God" (2 Corinthians 5:21).

> Believing, we rejoice
> To see the curse removed;
> We bless the Lamb with cheerful voice,
> And sing His bleeding love.

What curse?

The curse of the broken law; the curse of sin. Oh, what can be more wonderful than this: "We bless the Lamb with cheerful voice and sing His bleeding love!"

If you do not know that you are forgiven, by faith lay your hands upon that dear head of the Lamb of God, and like the penitent, confess your sin. Putting your faith in Him the curse will be removed from your heart and you will know your sin is forgiven because of the cleansing blood.

Which is He going to be for you—Savior or Judge?

If He is not your Savior, He must be your Judge.

The Bible does speak of certain ones who have sent their sins on before to judgment. By faith you can do that—send your sins on before. Have them judged and settled by His death. He forever put our sins where they cannot be found. Hear His voice of consolation and comfort and forgiveness today!